Mindset Blindspot

Why We Over-Please, Over-Think and Over-Work

Wanda van Gelderen

PAUL SMITH PUBLISHING
London

Published by Paul Smith Publishing London 2025

The stories in this book represent coaching and mentoring sessions with real people.
Some names have been changed at their request.

A CIP catalogue record for this title is available from the British Library
ISBN PB: 978-1-912597-51-2

ISBN eBook: 978-1-912597-52-9

Paul Smith Publishing
www.paulsmithpublishing.co.uk

To Douglas and Sarah

I love you to the moon and back. Wishing you both a life of no regrets, full of balance, joy, and success.

"Working with Wanda has been a genuinely transformative experience. She coached not only myself, but several members of my team, and the impact was both immediate and lasting. This book showcases Wanda's ability to challenge with empathy. She unlocks potential and creates space for real growth; supportive when needed, direct when it matters, and always insightful. Read this book if you want to become a better leader and a better version of yourself. With Wanda's coaching and guidance, I did just that!"

Andrew Dunbar, UK General Manager, SCC, and past Director, SoftwareOne.

"It had been ages since Wanda and I had spoken, so it was lovely to reconnect and catch up over a virtual coffee, as we often do these days. I was so impressed to hear about the book she'd been writing and especially surprised to learn that my research and work on mindset had been a key inspiration to her. I was beyond flattered and even more intrigued to read it. I recommend this highly accessible and relatable book to anyone wanting to learn more about mindset and eager to discover their blindspot."

Jodi O'Dell, CEO, Engage Coach International

"Who knew that high performance has a dark side? Reading this book was a revelation. It has illuminated the mindset blindspots behind my ambition and shown me how to turn this awareness into positive actions that allow me to being and to lead in a way that ensures I can enjoy a life of impact and no regrets. With its short engaging stories, this is an easy but powerful read that helps high performers enjoy growth and happiness and helps leaders of high performers provide the right support to their teams."

Melitta Campbell, Business Coach

Contents

Introduction

If you're looking to take charge of your life and go after what you want, this book is for you.

You'll meet inspiring people with invisible struggles. They are high achievers at work and appear to be flying, but internally, they feel stressed and stuck.

They are the mini version of the old me; driven, kind, and over-worked. Ten years ago, almost to the day of the first publication of this work, I had a heart attack. Life gave me a second chance, and a wake-up call!

I'll share my journey from being an overwhelmed over-achiever in the corporate world to becoming an internal coach in an IT company. Seven years in, I progressed to qualifying as a mindset coach.

Be the fly on the wall during my sessions to get a clear and deep understanding of yourself. Develop a passion for facing life head-on.

If you are reading this as a coach; this book will open your eyes to mindset coaching, but it won't make you pass a coaching exam. You'll see I am directive in places; I steer my clients when I feel it's helpful.

Mindset is a set of beliefs that shape how you see the world and yourself. It influences how you think, feel, and behave. It affects how you show up, both at work and at home. If you change your mindset, you change the results you get.

You'll realise we all have patterns of behaviour that sabotage us. Discover where you stand in your own way, as only from having this awareness can you move forward.

I will unveil a harsh truth: You have a Mindset Blindspot!

A blindspot occurs when your strengths become your weaknesses. What once got you praise or a promotion has turned into something you are over-doing, and now it is limiting your success.

You may recognise yourself. Are you over-doing your:

- Loyalty and commitment to work? Is it now disrupting your health and relationships?
- Drive for excellence? Has this turned into a harsh inner critic, which is now robbing you of joy and ease?
- Desire for harmony? Is your tendency to avoid conflict now trapping you in a people-pleasing mode?
- Craving for belonging? Is it making you work harder than you need to?
- Need to think things through? Have you developed a level of risk management that is now stopping you from taking the bold steps needed to thrive?

Your blindspot is why you have tendencies to be a people-pleaser, perfectionist and workaholic.

Why do we do the things we do? We want to belong, to be loved, and to be accepted. Our prehistoric hunter-gatherer brain, with its survival instinct, is still shaping our modern-day behaviour. We are hard-wired to work hard, help others and avoid risks to stay safe and alive. Our brains haven't caught up yet, that today we can be our authentic self and thrive.

This book will show you how to embrace the authentic you. You are enough.

Enjoy the amazing true stories of:

- Jack, who lost his motivation at work and after embracing his *Core Values* and tackling his over-thinking, found joy by helping and inspiring others.
- Hayley, who was over-worked because she readily volunteered for extra projects and believed that she should always be available. By using the *Eisenhower Matrix* and *Magic Quadrant,* she learned to delegate and created more work-life balance.
- Grace, who pleased her parents, and entered a profession she no longer wanted. *Journaling* helped her find the courage to break free and pursue her purpose.
- Alison, who got promoted and the first things she did was to find her team members' *Personality and Strengths.* We discovered when they were at their best.
- Natalie, who didn't know where to go next in her career, found that by embracing her *Zone of Genius,* stopped over-thinking and saw that the answer was right in front of her.
- Sharon, who built a business she loved. We studied her *Personality and Strengths* and aligned her offering and messaging, without burning out from over-work.
- Suki, who used my four questions in the *Stop, Keep, Start, Be Model* to get unstuck, and changed her career from being a coach to a university lecturer.
- Ilana, who exhausted herself by being a salami-slicer, aka people-pleaser. Hear how she's learnt from past mistakes, is promotion ready and more energetic.
- Anna, who used to put herself down and let guilt dictate her decisions, and by recognising her *Upper Limit Problem,* ditched people-pleasing for good.
- Caroline, who found that if your career path is no longer about the money, you make different choices. But when there are too many, procrastination can kick in.

- Paul, who was triple checking his work for fear of getting it wrong. By letting go of his need to be accurate, dedicated, and helpful, he relaxed and had space to grow.
- Adrian, an over-thinking high achiever, who could not decide whether to accept a promotion, until he asked himself; If not now, then when?
- Chantal, who was both confident and a harsh inner critic. She learnt to trust her decisions and tackle perfectionism by talking to herself as if she was a good friend.
- Sarah, who was over-committed and identified with her work achievements. She felt less overwhelmed the moment she gave herself some slack.
- Drishti, who called herself the misguided over-achiever, used my *Wheel of No Regrets* to get a push towards more self-care so that she could follow her dreams.

I have listed the stories so that you can dip in and out of this book whenever you identify with any of the situations above. The end of each chapter has a *Highlights* section to capture the essence of the story.

This book will create a deep understanding of yourself. You will learn what helps you and what hinders you in your pursuit of your goals.

Yes, you may start by having a mindset blindspot. But then, one day, the light comes on and you can see everything clearly. You will have the tools to create a life of no regrets, full of joy, purpose and success on your terms.

At the back of the book, you can find my simple, yet powerful, coaching resources.

I want everybody to have free access to this toolkit.

Step into a new beginning and move forward, fully alive. Be bold, trust yourself, and go after what you truly want.

It's time!

Download your Free Resources at **mindsetblindspot.com** or follow the QR Code

PART ONE:
MY WAKE-UP CALL

1

My Toughest Negotiation Yet

"Success is getting what you want.
Happiness is wanting what you get."

Dale Carnegie

"What do you mean, I can't get insurance? I thought you were the experts?"

I was stunned. All morning, my husband, Doug, and I had been ringing around to get travel insurance for our trip to the US.

"The thing is," the rep from the British Heart Foundation said, "people with Type 1 Diabetes and a recent heart attack are uninsurable for at least a year, possibly two years, depending on how they are doing. Second heart attacks are common."

I gulped. I couldn't believe what I was hearing.

"The combination of the two illnesses is very serious, and people can die," he continued. "A trip to the US without insurance is ill-advised. During an emergency, repatriation to the UK could cost £100,000."

"Well, we can't afford that, so we're not going to Disney World, and you can forget that business trip to Amsterdam, too," Doug declared. His tone signalled this was not up for discussion.

That telephone call frightened me. I relived my Type 1 Diabetes diagnosis and the heart attack that followed a few weeks later. My mind was racing. This is serious. I could die. Until then, death hadn't crossed my mind.

My overthinking kicked in. I was uninsurable. Nobody wants me. Does Doug still love me? Will I have a second heart attack?

I'd made a bucket list earlier that year and it included a trip to Disney World, Florida. In one swoop, this item was crossed off my list. It hurt, as I didn't want to disappoint my Disney-mad daughter, Sarah.

Another item on my list that year was an international role at work. I had just taken on a job at SoftwareOne, a global software reseller and services company, and discussions had started on how I could help build a global Procurement Service.

I knew I could do it. I'd spent the last twenty years working in IT Procurement and negotiated massive deals with the likes of Microsoft, Oracle and IBM. I had worked in corporates like Mobil Oil, Aviva, Bank of America, Barclays, Lloyds Banking Group and Citi. Every single one of these organisations was on the wish list of SoftwareOne.

Until that call, I felt I was on a roll. But a dark cloud had drifted in. What will they think at work if I don't go to Amsterdam? What will their reaction be that I can't fly for *two years*? I'm such a disappointment. My career is over!

My brain was in full overdrive, and I reminded myself of a magazine article I had read many years earlier about Kylie Minogue.

Doctors diagnosed her with breast cancer during her *Showgirl* tour. The magazine had a picture of her sitting on the floor, leaning against the railing of a luxury yacht. She was in a tracksuit, hunched over, arms wrapped around her knees, head bowed. She looked so sad and lost.

Even though I wasn't a massive fan of hers, that image was engrained in my mind. The article predicted that, following her diagnosis, she would start questioning everything in her life and her career could go down the drain. The article was right. Like a house of cards, everything came crashing down. She cancelled the tour, left her partner, and her singing career stalled.

Brace yourself, this could be you, I told myself. The thought of being like Kylie scared the hell out of me.

I, too, questioned everything from that day. If I died, what would happen? What would happen to Doug and Sarah? Are my finances in order? Would Doug be able to stay in the house? How would people remember me? Did I matter? Mortality became my motivation. I updated my will and put money aside for Sarah's university fees.

I also wondered about my career. Unwanted thoughts crowded my mind. All I could think of were things I didn't want:

I didn't want a UK-based job. It was too small.

I didn't want to take things easy. I was at the peak of my career.

I didn't want to die.

I wanted to thrive but didn't know how. I was stuck. None of the options on the table appealed, and I couldn't think straight. How was I going to back myself?

I could handle a £70 million Microsoft deal, but what I was facing here was my toughest negotiation yet.

The months that followed were full of inner turmoil. I didn't fully understand what was happening to my body, and I no longer trusted it. The pinpricks from my insulin needles became bruises because I was on blood thinners for my heart. My stomach area looked a mess.

My negative thoughts ended up sabotaging my happiness. Wrongly, I believed my appearance was disgusting. Somehow, I got it into my head that I was being punished for not being perfect. I became withdrawn at home and at work.

Books on happiness and the meaning of life were my constant companion. I was searching for an answer and was hoping for a quick fix. Of course, there was no quick fix.

I had briefly worked for Dale Carnegie Training and picked up an old copy of *How to Win Friends and Influence People*. This made me smile. Despite being decades old, most of the principles still applied. I realised that human nature doesn't change that much. We all need the same thing. We all want to be heard, seen, and understood.

It was time that I looked at the world through different coloured glasses. I went back to some old materials from Tony Robbins and his book *Awaken the Giant Within*. I knew I needed to improve my thought patterns if I was to create a compelling future. My inner work had started.

In a recent interview, Kylie Minogue explained that her cancer changed her life forever. She's become more grateful and appreciates what she's experienced. I smiled when I read that and thought about my past fears. It's not such a bad thing to be like her, after all.

2

What is My Legacy?

"Never give up."

Patrick Winter

I sat in the lobby of a London hotel, waiting for our CEO, Patrick. His flight from Geneva was late. I had been at SoftwareOne for less than four months and still felt like the new kid on the block. I was excited to be presenting at the mid-year sales conference.

As part of the conference, employees could book a ten-minute slot with Patrick. Few took the opportunity, but I went for it. We hadn't met yet, and I was eager to discuss my thoughts on offering negotiation support to customers involved in deals with IBM and Oracle.

SoftwareOne already offered contract optimisation support for customers with Microsoft deals, and I believed we could expand the business if we did the same for other large vendors.

"Come in, come in," he said with a smile, ushering me into a tiny meeting room with open arms. "So sorry I'm late, trouble with the flight, and it was a long drive from the airport."

His strong Swiss accent caught me by surprise. Patrick had a tall frame and his gestures were warm. He wore a light-coloured linen shirt, red jeans and white trainers. I had never seen a Corporate CEO wearing trainers. His attire captivated me.

I assumed he spent little time outside the German-speaking market and that he didn't have time to get changed. I later learned that I was wrong on both counts. It just shows that you cannot judge a book by its cover.

In front of us, on the table, sat a large platter under a stainless-steel dome. Patrick had to dash out and I couldn't help myself. I stood up and lifted the dome to uncover what lay beneath. I unveiled a stunning plate of fruit, cut into bite-size chunks, presented in a pretty pattern. It had every colour of the rainbow. I quickly put the dome back, my heart racing, not wanting to be caught in the act.

Patrick returned moments later and said, "I heard about you. How are you settling in?"

"Well, I've had a bit of a bumpy start," I said. "I have been off for a couple of weeks. I had a heart attack. But I'm all well now and ready to go."

"Say that again!? A heart attack?"

"Yes."

"My father had one too, not that long ago. Either stressful events or underlying health conditions cause heart attacks."

What a strange response, I thought. It seemed like he needed to explain what he was hearing.

"What happened to my father made me decide to lead a healthy life."

Hence the fruit, I thought. He still hadn't lifted the dome.

"I watch my diet, run, and play tennis. I have no regrets in life. If my time was up, I would have one more game of tennis."

I totally got why Patrick impressed so many people. The man was larger than life and oozed confidence. You felt an irresistible urge to be part of his dream to expand his business. His goal was to have an office in every country. As I write this, SoftwareOne has offices in over eighty.

The UK arm of the business was about seven years old when I joined. During my interview, Zak, the UK MD, told me about how he'd met Patrick and how his vision for a global business had motivated him.

I knew Zak from old. I met him through Garry, a mutual business connection and friend. They came to visit me when I ran the Global Software Procurement Team at Barclays Investment Bank. I loved Zak's optimism.

SoftwareOne UK was in its first year of trading, and despite being a tiny player in the market, Zak wanted to discuss how he could become a supplier of Microsoft licences to the bank. There was no way I could appoint SoftwareOne, but from that moment, I kept my eye on them.

After I left the bank, I became an independent consultant and offered my services to several other banks that were managing large Microsoft renewals. Time and time again, the advisory team at SoftwareOne blew me out of the water. No other Microsoft partner had such a knowledgeable group of people.

Phil, a co-founder, intrigued me when he approached me to join the company. I liked the company but wasn't sure where I might fit in. "We'll sort something out. You can help us grow. That is all that matters," I was told.

I loved that philosophy, and it made for a great experience working for SoftwareOne. I had several roles in the business, and I was truly fortunate to work with Zak and his leadership team. They saw my transferable skills, and they gave me the flexibility to do the work that I loved.

The UK became one of the most successful offices outside of the German-speaking region and grew to over two hundred people. In preparation for this book, I asked Zak what made the UK such a success, and he told me, "We started the business in my living room. I handpicked several key individuals from the industry. The UK was a tough market to enter, as it already had several established companies.

Key to our success was our ability to identify the gap in the market and have a team that could pivot on its offering to leverage the opportunity. Through heavy lobbying within Microsoft, we showed how we could drive renewals aligned to customers' future growth and deployment aspirations."

The UK became the seventh country and Zak opened Ireland, Sweden, Finland, and South Africa. I saw the brilliance in Zak and his team's work. They took their window of opportunity, with Patrick by their side.

Patrick placed people first, realizing that happy staff meant happy customers.

He would say things such as

Treat everyone with fairness, compassion, and respect.

Start every day with a thank you email.

Be generous with your time.

It's not work if you love what you do.

You cannot change the past. Tomorrow is not a promise, so live now in the moment, as this is all you can control.

Never give up.

Sometimes you win, sometimes you lose.

Sadly, three years after I met Patrick, he passed away after of an accident whilst on holiday. It came as a complete shock, catching the entire company off guard.

The unenviable task of delivering the news fell to Zak. I will never forget the moment we sat in a huddle on the ground floor in the Wimbledon office and heard that Patrick required life support in a Spanish hospital. It's like remembering where you were when you learned about John Lennon's shooting or the collapse of the New York Twin Towers.

The news hit us like a ton of bricks. It was impossible to know what to say.

One day, when Zak did his rounds on the floor, I said to him, "You know Patrick had no regrets in life, don't you? I hope knowing this will help." He responded, "Patrick lived life to the full and impacted so many people. Patrick's key ability was that he hired the right people. He found those individuals who would go above and beyond and put the customer first. It was always the winning formula. He backed his team."

It was difficult to grasp the loss of Patrick. The effect on Zak and his leadership team was immense. He had not only lost a leader but also a friend, mentor, and confidant. The company was never the same after that.

The chairperson of the board stepped in to fill Patrick's role and then, within three months, a new CEO assumed the position.

Patrick's hard work primed the company to go public. Within the next twelve month's SoftwareOne acquired one of its biggest global competitors, Comparex and then in the following six months listed on the Swiss Stock Exchange.

After Patrick's passing, the team created something in his memory. There is a wall in the Wimbledon office that captures a large photo of him together with his philosophy. His influence still resonates deeply with those who knew him. Under the photo is says I have no regrets in life. If my time was up, I would have one more game of tennis.

I call this his *Legacy Wall.*

Someone's death can trigger reflections on your own legacy. Patrick's passing made me ponder the nature of my lasting impact.

I'd climbed the ladder in the first twenty years of my IT Procurement career. I now call this my *building phase*. It served me and my family well. I poured everything into my work, saying yes to every opportunity, pushing harder, and constantly looking ahead to the next step. I was fuelled by ambition and was proud of my accomplishment. It was all about moving up and building my reputation.

But becoming seriously ill had changed my focus. I started moving into my *being phase*. I started asking different questions. Bigger questions. What am I really doing all this for? What impact am I leaving behind? How do I want to be remembered?

The *being phase* is less about climbing and more about meaning. It's about stepping back, reassessing what truly matters, and finding joy in the journey, not just the destination. Work is still important, but it's no longer the only thing. Instead of just building a career, I wanted to build a legacy - something that would last beyond job titles and company achievements.

Moving from the *building phase* to the *being phase* wasn't a sudden change. It happened over many years. But once I embraced it, everything felt different. It wasn't about doing more; it was about doing what mattered. I let go of the idea that success had to mean constant striving and instead started looking for ways to create an impact in a way that felt right for me.

Being confronted with death made me read about the topic. My favourite book is *The Top Five Regrets of the Dying* by Bronnie Ware. The audible version has nine hours of Bronnie's recollections of her work as an end-of-life nurse. She recalls the deep conversations she had with her palliative patients. Bronnie was excellent at listening, and this allowed her patients to be honest about their impending departure.

Bronnie's voice is soothing, and her stories are both sad and funny and interlaced with her own struggles in life. The book shows how when people have little to lose, they become free from societal pressures and empowered to speak their minds.

Bronnie found that our Top Five Regrets are:

1. I wish I'd the courage to live a life true to myself, not the life others expected of me.
2. I wish I hadn't worked so hard.
3. I wish I'd had the courage to express my feelings.
4. I wish I had stayed in touch with my friends.
5. I wish I had let myself be happier.

I think Bronnie created a perfect foundation for what it means to have lived well. I took Bronnie's findings and started exploring what it meant to have no regrets.

Remembering Patrick and seeing the creation of the *Legacy Wall* solidified my thoughts. My legacy has nothing to do with my death, but with how I live now.

My legacy is the wisdom I share with those around me, the examples I set and the inspirational things I do. Helping others to live a life of no regrets is my impact.

It's time to change the world, one person at a time.

3

Conquering Fear, One Step at a Time

"Above all, have the courage to follow your heart and your intuition. Everything else is secondary. Our hearts know what our longings are. What truly matters."

Steve Jobs

I removed my shoes and socks and listened to the announcements: "It is safe to leave all your belongings under your chair. Please leave everything behind and make a mental note of your seating section and row so you can find your chair later. Let's go!"

I felt sick. There was no going back. Thousands of strangers surrounded me, and we all snaked slowly out of the building into the car park. Everybody had bare feet. It was a late afternoon in February, and it was dark. As soon as we entered the car park, we saw it had been cleared of cars and replaced by row upon row of hot coals.

I stared in disbelief at about twenty rows of hot coals. Each took up two car parking spaces in length. I spoke under my breath as I shuffled forward towards the coals, "Oh shit, oh shit, oh shit. Stay calm and do your power move. You can do this."

There were so many people that I couldn't see the coals anymore. We were queueing up, and all I could hear was, "Move along. Let's go!"

As I moved along, I could feel the heat of the coals on my right. I must have reached the tenth row of coals as an assistant manoeuvred me away from the long snake and lined me up in front of the coals. It was my turn soon. Maybe twenty people were ahead of me, and the line was moving quickly. Too quickly. "Swoosh…! Swoosh...! Swoosh...!" I called out, doing my power move.

I was moving my arms fast from the top of my shoulders in an X shape down to my hips. As my arms lowered the "Swoosh…!" was called out. Others were calling out "Yes…! Yes...! Yes...!" or "Go...! Go...! Go...!". Each of us had our own power move and each of us was in our own world as we moved forward.

I stood in that car park more than twenty years ago at Tony Robbins' UPW event in London. The *Unleash the Power Within* programme, has Tony, the world-renowned life coach and motivational speaker, on stage in front of thousands of people.

Tony was my first exposure to the power of coaching. The simplicity of it balled me over. He took us through three intense days of utter magic. I came away with some much inspiration. He had showed me that *my state,* the feelings and thoughts in the moment, could change my perspective on things. I learned that fear was the main reason for getting stuck. If you can overcome fear, magical things happen.

In the years after my heart attack, fear became my primary driver. Every minor setback in my health frightened me. At one point, I had two frozen shoulders. I was sleep deprived and unable to get dressed without help from Doug. Movement became difficult, and it all ended up with a denervation treatment in my back. No wonder I was stuck.

I needed to do something. I spoke to a coach. Rachel was an American and didn't know me. I didn't want anybody to know that I was having this conversation.

"I want to know about your heart attack. Why don't you tell me about it?"

"There isn't much to tell," I piped up. "It's ages ago, and I only found out four days after the event that I'd had a heart attack. So, no real drama. I didn't even call 999."

"999?"

"The emergency services," I explained.

"Well, that's interesting," Rachel said. "Tell me more."

"I didn't know I'd had a heart attack. I had chest pains, but didn't collapse to the floor with it, like in the movies."

"Didn't it hurt?"

"It hurt like hell. I had been to a boot camp in the morning. Afterwards, I went home and had to lie down. I remember crying in bed."

"So, what was going on?" I could hear that Rachel had softened her voice to show that she had picked up on my slight embarrassment.

"You see, there is a bit of history here. I'd already been to the hospital about five times in the previous couple of months. Every time we had to wait for hours, and my husband joked about knowing every coffee machine in the Accident and Emergency Department."

"And?"

"I didn't want to bother anyone."

“Okay…” There was a nod and a pause.

“Also, the doctors found nothing, so it felt pointless to go again.”

After a brief pause, Rachel asked, “What else could have been going on?”

“Well, we had my husband’s work party in the evening. We had booked an overnight stay in a fancy hotel. If I ended up in hospital, we would have missed the party.”

“Anything else…?”

“You shouldn’t call an ambulance for minor stuff,” I declared.

Rachel had picked up on my deep-seated emotions of not feeling deserving. She also pointed out that I was using language such as *should*. This showed that I had made myself a set of rules. They were not helpful. She suggested that my generalisation about doctors not finding anything didn’t empower me to take control of my health.

I discovered that deep in my subconscious, limiting beliefs were at play. I had put myself on the second row, and it could have cost me my life.

I’m truly grateful for that coaching session. It was my trigger to become a coach myself. It was a wake-up call. Addressing limiting beliefs became a bit of an obsession. I started spotting them and developed questioning techniques to unearth them.

I longed for great coaching sessions, like the one I had with Rachel. I was ready for deep conversations about fears and dreams. I wanted to help people get out of their way and discover how their lives could be better - much better.

So, you may wonder, what happened in that London car park twenty years ago?

When it was my turn, I was so prepared that it didn't enter my mind to back out. I followed the person before me and stepped onto the hot coals. I didn't count the steps, but it must have been around eight steps. Eight steps of sheer terror, done in a trance. It was over in a flash.

Straight after, a man holding a fire hose shouted, "Lift your foot and the other one!" The ice-cold water hit the bottom of my feet, and the man checked between my toes. "Well done. Please return to the hall!" he bellowed out.

The tarmac felt rough, and my feet were sore. On my way back to the hall, staff members lined the route, jumping up and down, smiling, giving high fives, and shouting, "Well done! You did it! Amazing!"

After what felt like a very long walk, I returned to my seat and hugged the stranger beside me. I had faced my fear. I checked my feet, and to my surprise, there was no damage. Then it sunk in; Holy moly, I had done my first fire walk!

PART TWO
INTRODUCTION TO COACHING

4

Find Your Core Values

"Success usually comes to those who
are too busy to be looking for it."

Henry Thoreau

I was sitting opposite Jack in our Wimbledon office. The first thing I noticed was the shock of blond curls and the twinkle in his eyes. He was tall, athletic, and had a broad smile. The quality of his shirt was a sign he liked the finer things in life. He was part of our high-potential programme, and I was his internal coach.

I liked Jack. He was enthusiastic and always willing to help. He also understood the power of coaching. His mother was a Leadership Coach.

As we settled, I asked, "What's on your mind?"

"In the last few months, I have put in little effort. I have lost my mojo."

"What makes you say that?" I asked.

"I lost a big sale and, deep down, I know we didn't deserve the business because we couldn't deliver. I'm not convinced by our product."

"What else is on your mind?"

"The red tape and people around me drain me. There is so much negative energy it's beyond a joke."

"Well, they say you are the average of the five people you hang out with, so be selective about who you work with." I smiled and thought to myself how Jack would be the perfect addition to my five at work.

"Anything else?"

"I used to smash my targets. I loved it. I would imagine sitting on a beach sipping cocktails with my girlfriend, and that was enough to get me going. I have noticed that having more stuff or booking another holiday no longer motivates me."

As I listened, I noticed his low energy and considered how to lift his spirits.

"What do you want to use this session for?" I asked.

"Between you and me, I'm considering my options," Jack said. "I'm wondering whether being in sales is what I want. I live on an eternal rollercoaster, and I want off."

"Tell me about this rollercoaster."

Jack pondered for a few seconds and said, "When I started my career, I liked the highs of commission payments. They were worth the lows of the hard work and long hours. It didn't bother me that every year my sales target would get bigger. I would earn more, and that was great."

"Go on."

"But now, the highs are too brief and the lows too long. The top of the ride is when I'm most driven to sell, and the bottom of the ride is when I'm stuck, and I'm over-thinking."

"Where are you now?"

"At the bottom of the ride. I'm considering if something else rather than commission is my motivator. Right now, all these questions are circling in my mind. Ultimately, I want to rekindle my passion for my work," Jack responded.

"How about I can help you figure out what is really important to you," I said.

"That would be great."

I explained to Jack that I use an exercise called *Find Your Core Values* to help figure out what drives and motivates people. It's a concept by Stan Slap.

You may want to do this exercise too. You will find it at the back of the book, under **Resources.**

I said to Jack, "Please have a look at these twenty-nine words and consider:

What describes you best?

What did you learn from your parents?

What were you like at school?

How would your best friend describe you?"

"Let me have a look," Jack responded.

I asked, "Please write down the ten words that appeal the most. There are no right or wrong answers. You already live by these principles and have probably done so for most of your adult life. This is not about who you want to be in the future. This is about who you are already."

"Okay," Jack said. "What happens if I have a core value that's not in this list?"

"If there are words that are missing, there is a row of blank boxes so that you can add your own."

"Got it," Jack smiled. "I've selected my ten words."

I continued, "Now cross out four and reduce the list down to six. Remove words that are similar or less important to you. Keep the six words that motivate you to be the best version of yourself. Don't think too much when selecting your six. What comes to your mind first will be the clearest sign of your values. Ask yourself:

Does this value boost my self-esteem?

Am I proud of it?

Would it feel okay to share this with others?

Does it represent things I would support, even if my choice isn't popular or would put me in the minority?"

"Now that last question is an excellent test. That makes things much clearer," Jack said. "Based on that, my six words are Advancement, Fun, Learning, Passion and I would add Authenticity and Optimism."

"The next step of the exercise is to reduce the list of six down to your final three. These are what I call your *Top Core Values*. These are the things you stand for, the things you would fight for, and the things that would upset you if they were missing in your life."

"Mine are Advancement, Learning and Fun," Jack said.

"Now that we know your top three, we can reflect on how these show up in your life. Because they are important, they drive you at work and bring joy to you and to those around you. However, there is also a dark side to your core values. Because they are so important to you, you are in danger of overdoing them. Maybe you get very upset when they are missing."

"Makes sense," Jack said.

" Let's discuss advancement. What joy does it bring to you and when is the dark side showing?"

"Advancement makes me self-motivated and hardworking. I've been an over-achiever from a young age. I suppose at work that shows up through the numbers. I normally hit or exceed my targets."

"What about the dark side? What happens when advancement is missing?"

"That's where I'm now. The high-potential programme gave no promises, but it did make me wonder about potential leadership roles. I want to progress, but the organisation is flat so there are no promotion opportunities. When advancement is missing, I'm getting restless. I sense I'm not achieving enough," Jack explained.

“Are you overdoing your need for advancement?”

“Maybe.”

“What about learning?” I continued. “What does your desire for learning give you and those around you, and what happens when it’s missing?”

“It’s very similar to advancement. I love learning new things and will always seek to grow. I’m curious and have an interest in new things. Again, when it’s missing, I get bored and restless. I’m stagnating. I hate it.”

“On what side of learning do you consider yourself to be today?”

“Definitely the dark side,” Jack said with a smile.

“To finish, let’s talk about fun,” I said. “Same question. What does having fun as your core value give you and those around you, and what happens when it is missing?”

“I’m a fun guy, both at work and at home. It’s important to me to keep things light and have fun colleagues and friends. When it’s missing, I’m miserable. Life is too short to be serious all the time.”

“I couldn’t agree more,” I smiled. “Doing this exercise has shown us that advancement, learning and fun are important right now. They give you joy, meaning, and purpose. If you can attract more of this in your work, I’m convinced your mojo will return. What could you do to bring them back?”

“That’s the thing. I’m not sure if I’m making much headway with advancement. Despite hitting 160% of my target last year, I cannot see me climbing the ladder. I wonder if I’m outgrowing my role and should consider for a more challenging environment?”

"Yes, you could consider that. What about learning? How can you pull that into your day-to-day activities?"

"I'm not learning much myself, but I do like helping others to grow," Jack said. "I hear that there's an opportunity to become a mentor. I might investigate that. Also, I think I could help with sales training. I will have a chat with the training department."

"Great idea. What about the fun side?"

"Training would be fun. I would like to become a sales trainer one day. Also, there is a new product we are selling. It's complex and I like the sales specialist. I could learn from him and add a bit more fun that way."

In the months that followed, Jack applied for Sales Manager positions outside the company. The roles came with an intense selection process and preparing for interviews energised him. It gave him a positive boost.

He also became a mentor and started doing some sales training. He had stopped thinking about his sales target and concentrated instead on helping and inspiring others.

Here is the twist. His sales performance increased, and he achieved 250% of his target the following year. He started hanging out with people he respected and could learn from and sold complex and high-end solutions. I was proud when Jack got invited to present at our quarterly sales meeting about how he had done so well.

He also got offered a new job. The offer was tempting, but Jack didn't take it. Instead, he made a bold move. He was on his honeymoon in Africa, and together with his new wife, he decided that life was too short and that they would spend the next six months travelling the world. He followed his heart and embraced what he cared about - things that are genuine, enjoyable, and exciting.

After he returned from his travels, Jack took a job as Commercial Director at his mother's business. He's now doing sales training with an emphasis on finding your intrinsic motivation.

Highlights

- You are the average of the five people you spend time with, so be selective about who you hang out with.
- Knowing your core values helps you to understand what drives you and what inspires you.
- Your top core values bring you joy, meaning, and purpose.
- However, there is also a dark side to your core values. Because they are so important to you, you are in danger of overdoing them.
- You can stop over-thinking by concentrating on helping and inspiring others.

5

Aim For the Magic Quadrant

"The key is not to prioritize what's on your schedule, but to schedule your priorities."

Stephen Covey

Like Jack, Hayley was part of the SoftwareOne high-potential programme. She used our coaching to hone her leadership skills, after she was promoted to manager of the internal sales team.

You couldn't miss Hayley. She had a larger-than-life personality and was warm, fun-loving, and friendly. I admired her ability to be herself; a strong and colourful woman in a man's world.

She tied her dark red hair back and wore big silver looped earrings. Heavy eyeliner and false eyelashes made her green eyes pop. Her bright red lipstick, which matched the colour of her manicured nails, enhanced her big smile.

She had an elaborate tattoo on the back of her neck, *ARCHIE*. She had a grey flower tattooed on her right shoulder and another one on her thigh. Her left calf had a picture of a deer with her fawn. On her right calf, she had a fox head with a garland of flowers. These tattoos weren't random images. They were all connected to people in her life. Family was everything to Hayley.

Hayley was a single mum to her five-year-old son, Archie. She often talked about Archie's antics. It entertained us to no end. He became part of the SoftwareOne family. Archie knew my name and those of the other team members.

At that time, SoftwareOne operated very much like a family business. Staff members were hand-picked, and loyalty was both expected and given. It didn't matter what your job was, everybody mucked in and supported the cause. We all had the same vision; we wanted to grow and be the best in the industry.

The Wimbledon office had a large open plan seating arrangement. The inside sales team sat along the southern wall, where large windows flooded the desks with light. Hayley sat in the middle of the first row of desks. It was like a parent sitting at the top of a large dining table. Hearing and seeing everything and being in charge.

There was a lot of chatter between team members, and Hayley was always on hand to shout out the answer to a question that was being discussed. She was knowledgeable, highly skilled, and loved ticking off tasks. All she wanted was a happy team and delighted customers. No wonder SoftwareOne invited her to the over-achievers' President's Club, year after year.

When the COVID-19 pandemic hit, we all worked from home. With the schools closed, Archie was home, too. It was an impossible situation. He was too young to be left on his own. Hayley's productivity plummeted.

On one of our coaching calls, Archie sat next to her on the couch, notepad in hand and wanting to *join in.* Hayley wanted to have a serious conversation with me, but Archie was not having any of it. He wanted to have fun. He soon got bored and asked for a sandwich and his iPad. His mum quickly obliged.

"I've lost total control over the situation. If I don't laugh, I'd cry."

"How are you and Archie doing?"

"The school is still closed and there is nothing I can do about it. I fret about work when relaxing with Archie in the evening, so as soon as he goes to bed, I return to my laptop. I have nothing else to do and I feel working late is better than dealing with a long to-do list in the morning."

"You need a man in your life," I joked.

"One day," Hayley replied. "Archie is the only man in my life right now."

"And how is your team doing?"

"They are fine. It's hard for some of them to work from home, because they are sitting at the family kitchen table or in their bedroom. I'm constantly available on Instant Messaging to help with queries."

"Are your team leads not picking this up?" I asked.

"Yes, they are, but I'm also helping. You know me, I like to stay in control," Hayley smiled.

"Yes, I know. But you're sinking. Why don't you delegate?" I asked.

"It's quicker to do it myself. It's in my blood. I never stop."

"What's in your blood?"

"I was born a grafter. Just like my dad. He's a labourer and earns an honest day's living. I help him with his books after work. We are there for each other and always will be. I'm happiest when I get a lot done," Hayley said.

"Okay. Can you tell me about a typical day? This week, for example, what have you been working on?"

"I always spend the first few hours on firefighting. Queries from our internal team in India and customers."

"It sounds like you do the important and urgent tasks first. That's great. It reminds me of Stephen Covey. He talks about 'Put First Things First.' Covey got his ideas from the *Eisenhower Matrix*, a time management tool, designed by Dwight Eisenhower, the 34th President of the United States," I said. I showed Hayley the matrix.

You can find the *Eisenhower Matrix* in the **Resources** section at the end of this book.

"You've got Quadrant One nailed. This is the urgent and important piece. What about Quadrant Two? Do you spend any time on planning and pro-active work?"

"Not enough," Hayley responded straight away. I'd love to, but I simply don't have the time."

"The *Eisenhower Matrix's* top right-hand box is also known as the *Magic Quadrant.* Move to the top right-hand side of the Matrix and you will feel on top of the world, calm and in control."

"That's cool," Hayley nodded.

"The best way to make sure you have time for planning is to schedule it in your diary. Call it your 'Board Meeting', if you want to signify its importance. This meeting needs to happen no matter what."

"That's a good idea," Hayley smiled. "I will update my diary tonight."

"What about Quadrant Three? This is the delegation box."

Hayley laughed. "I suppose I need to get better at this."

"You are very short on time, now that you have Archie at home, so let's have a look at how your team leads can pick up more," I suggested. "Are there things that you don't need to get involved in?"

"They can handle most things," Hayley replied. "It's just the escalations that are tricky. I need to get involved in those."

"Fair enough. How can you make sure that you don't get involved too early?"

Hayley thought for a while, "I can make sure that only the team leads escalate to me, rather than all and sundry. That way, I empower my team leads, and I reduce the noise I get."

"That sounds like a double win," I smiled. "What else could you delegate?"

"I wonder whether I can pass on some of the training I do," Hayley pondered. "I volunteered to be a global trainer for the new sales system, and that's taking up far more time than I expected."

"What made you volunteer for that?"

"The UK team was in the first wave of the role out, and we did really well, so it's nice to be asked."

"But haven't you already volunteered for lots of other projects?"

"Yes, I have. Hindsight is a good thing, isn't it? Maybe I was a bit too keen and now I'm paying the price."

"Yes, you are," I smiled. "Shall we have a look at Quadrant Four? Is there anything you can delete from your to-do-list. Are there things you can stop doing? Could you eliminate distractions? How much time are you spending looking at your phone, for example, or chatting with people?"

"I do like a good catch up," Hayley grinned. "I'll watch that one!"

During the months after this session, Hayley rigorously used the *Eisenhower Matrix* to get better at time management and delegation.

She no longer works in the evenings and has taken up weightlifting at a friend's gym. Most importantly, Archie can join in, too.

Highlights

- Over-work comes from always volunteering for extra projects.
- It's not helping if you believe you must always be available and responsive.
- Work-life balance disappears when you work late nights and weekends to stay on top of work.
- The over-worked lose themselves, as their job consumes their identity.
- The *Eisenhower Matrix* is an excellent tool for figuring out what to do first, what to schedule and what to delegate.
- Schedule your important work and spend time in your *Magic Quadrant*, to feel calm and in control.

6

Choose Your Path by Journaling

"Dream no small dreams, for they have no power to move the hearts of men."

Victor Hugo

"I've had enough… When it gets tough, it gets brutal. Parents can be nasty, and kids are unappreciative. I've done this for eight years and I'm finding it really tough."

Opposite me sat a head of department from an inner-city school. She was an attractive woman in her early thirties, with beautiful long chestnut hair. Her clothes, eyebrows, white teeth, and manicured nails showed she looked after herself. She had a wide smile and the deepest, richest brown eyes. Her voice had a soft tone, and she articulated her words.

I warmed to her instantly.

This was my first coaching session with Grace. Her mind was whirling, and she had lost some of her confidence. She wanted to regain her inner strength.

"Tell me about your work?"

"I work with children who've grown up in one of the poorest cities in the country. Even though I run a department, pastoral duties fill most of my day," Grace said. "They promoted me year after year. My colleagues respect me, and I'm not sure if my pupils do."

What a kind and brilliant woman, I thought.

"What got you into teaching?"

My parents were teachers, and they wanted to best for me. They would tell me: "The best way to be in a proper job that is respectable and stable is to be in teaching." So, that's what I did.

"And you've had enough?"

"Yes!"

"It's not uncommon to follow in your parents' footsteps. I'm wondering how often it has a happy outcome," I pondered.

I've become so resentful of my job and so desperate to leave that I've just handed in my notice without having another job to go to."

"Wow, that's quite something," I said.

"I'm exhausted and want to take back control. I don't know what I'm going to do next, but I've got three months to work things out. I hope you can help me with that."

"Of course. Where do you want to start?"

"I haven't told my parents yet. I don't want to let them down, but I can't stand teaching. I can no longer do this. It's killing me."

"Can you describe your parents to me?"

"Well, they're teachers and always know best. They have an opinion on everything and have a map of my life drawn out, even though I'm an adult now."

"So, now you don't know how to tell them your news?"

"That's it. I'm dreading it. How on earth am I going to tell my parent that their path is no longer mine?"

"What's worrying you?"

"I was a quiet and agreeable child. I feel torn. On the one hand, I want to be confident, and on the other, I feel like this agreeable child again. Subservient and over-pleasing. Also, I don't even know what I want to do next. I'm so stressed I cannot think straight. I need to get to the end of term."

"How would you like to feel when you meet your parents?"

"Calm and clear," Grace said softly, "And brave."

"From what I can see, you are brave. Why don't we focus on creating calm and getting to the end of term?"

"Yes, please."

'Let's take things slower. We don't have to figure everything out in one session," I explained.

I suggested that journaling could help her manage this phase. I use three different journals, and you can find more information in the **Resources** section at the back of the book.

Celebration Journal

Write down your small wins as they happen to you. These are all the positive things, successes and celebrations. Read this journal on the days you don't feel it. This will keep you grounded and prepare you for when you must face challenges. This journal allows you to avoid the rollercoaster feeling of having highs and lows.

Evidence Journal

Record any sign that shows you that you're going in the right direction towards your goals. Write down things you see (e.g. adverts / other people's behaviour). Reading the content will lift you up. Write in the journal as soon as the evidence happens and capture the feelings in that moment (do not wait until long after as the intensity of the feeling won't be there).

BHAG Journal

BHAG stands for Big Hairy Audacious Goals. These are the dreams you cannot calculate. The things that seem so far out there, that you don't know how to make it come true. What would you do if you knew you couldn't fail? What's your bold vision? The reason for this journal is to flex your dream muscles. Most of us don't dream big enough.

In the following days, Grace practised expressing her genuine emotions. She would not only have to announce her news, but possibly also defend her actions. Journaling helped her stand firm in her decision. The discussion with her parents wasn't as terrifying as she thought. They were more interested in what Grace would do next and, as always, wanted the best for her.

In her BHAG Journal, Grace wrote about working for a local law firm. She passed the interviews with flying colours and joined the firm of her dreams.

Highlights

- Journalling is not about writing but about letting your thoughts flow freely, without judgement.
- By writing down your thoughts and fears, you will recognise patterns in your thinking.
- A celebration journal captures your small wins, as they happen. By living in the moment, you gain perspective, and it shows that you are capable. It boosts your confidence.
- An evidence journal allows you to reflect on what lessons you have learned and document evidence you are getting closer to your goals. Read the journal on the days that you are not at your best. The content will lift you.
- The BHAG journal is for your exciting dreams and adventures. Write down what gets you going. These are the dreams that seem so far out there, that you do not know how to make them come true. This is not about things. This is about what makes you feel alive. It encourages you to dream big. Most of us don't dream big enough.

7

Discover Your Strengths and Happy Head

"Happiness is when what you think, what you say, and what you do are in harmony."

Mahatma Gandhi

I grew up in the Netherlands, and as a child, my dad gave me the nickname *Little Sarah,* or *Saartje* in Dutch. It was after a character in a very popular children's TV series called Swiebertje. The weekly programme entertained the nation with the antics of an innocent tramp, his ongoing arguments with police officer Bromsnor, and his hidden love for Saartje, the mayor's housekeeper.

Saartje was agreeable, helpful, kind, organised, and hard-working. My dad chose this nickname well. I had the same characteristics as the sweet housekeeper. I was a kind and happy kid who kept her room tidy, and I loved helping my mum around the house. My personality was noticeable from a young age and didn't change much as I grew older.

Those same personality traits would later predict what would make me stressed at work. I have always hated conflict, unhelpfulness, and cruelty. I would do anything to create order and harmony.

Have you ever wondered what makes you happy and what makes you stressed?

Maybe you are happiest when you feel that you're making a difference at work, or when you have a detailed plan when you go on holiday. These examples point to aspects of your personality.

Do you want to find out what your personality type is?

Please go to the **Resources** section at the back of this book, to find a link to a free personality test. The test will give you your *Myers-Briggs Type Indicator* (or MBTI) results.

I'm trying to remember when I first heard about the MBTI personality test. It must have been when I studied Applied Psychology at the University of Surrey. It's scary how time flies.

My Myers-Briggs Type Indicator is an INFJ.

What is yours?

MBTI measures four aspects of your personality.

First, where do you get your energy from? The scale shows extraversion (E) on the one hand and introversion (I) on the other. Your score shows where on the continuum your preference is. E's focus on the external world and get energised by interacting with people. I's, on the other hand, focus on the internal world, and prefer to do things independently.

For example, my personality type is a strong introvert. I'm a home bird and love spending time on my own. Large groups exhaust me. However, I can act as an extrovert when invited to a friend's birthday party and have a lovely time. I just can't pull an all-nighter.

Second, MBTI measures how you solve problems and take in information. Do you prefer concrete facts and detail (Sensing or S), or do you rather look for patterns and high-level information (Intuition or N)?

Third, MBTI measures how you make decisions. Do you prefer to make decisions with your heart (Feeling or F) or your head (Thinking or T)?

I make my decisions with my heart. That is how I ended up buying a flat with a living room in the shape of a turret. I loved the idea of living in a tower. However, after I bought it, I learnt that the building was over a hundred years old and would be costly to maintain.

My husband, Doug, on the other hand, is a strong T. He's an engineer. Everything he does, at work and at home, is based on logic, measurements or data. He keeps my feet firmly on the ground.

Lastly, MBTI measures how you generally approach life. Those on the judging (J) end of the scale prefer structure and plans, while those on the perceiving (P) side prefer flexibility and keeping options open.

I'm a J through and through and love a plan. I'm very task-oriented and make a list of things to do. I like to get my work done before relaxing. I plan my work to avoid rushing just before a deadline.

I used the MBTI exercise with my client Alison. Alison had recently been promoted to Sales Director. I had coached her before her promotion, and she was familiar with the MBTI tool.

In the first month of her new role, Alison asked her team members to take the quick test, and she asked permission to share the results with the team. Of course, everybody was up for it. Alison also made a personal information pack for each team member. It was a fun and light-hearted exercise that allowed team members to learn about themselves and others.

Each pack contained the individual results and a summary of what the test results meant. The report listed strengths and weaknesses of each team member. There was also a list of famous people with the same personality. The sharing of famous people was a hit in the group feedback session.

This exercise had two major benefits for Alison. First, early in her tenure, she quickly got to know each of her team members on a deep level. This allowed her to allocate work in a way that reflected team members' strengths and happiness.

Second, it showed the team that she cared about them and that she was investing in personal development. It cost nothing but time, but the gesture is worth its weight in gold.

Happy Head and *Stress Head* are fun, modern additions to the MBTI toolkit. They help you see how your personality type affects your moods and reactions.

Happy Head is when you feel good, use your natural strengths, and cruise through life with contentment. It's when everything feels balanced. It's when you are relaxed and at your best.

Stress Head, on the other hand, is when things aren't going so smoothly. It's when stress takes over, and you act in ways that aren't typical for you, leading to feelings of anxiety and frustration.

Recognising whether you are in a *Happy Head* or *Stress Head* state can help you manage your stress and return to a better place. You can navigate life's ups and downs more effectively, leading to personal growth and better relationships.

So, how can you find out what your *Happy Head* and *Stress Head* look like?

Go to the **Resources** section at the back of this book to find the link to the MBTI site.

Each head has around thirty phrases or words that make you happy or stressed, depending on whether you are looking at your *Happy Head* or *Stress Head*. Some phrases are bold, others are small, and others are big. None of this relates to the meaning of the words. I suggest you read all the words and select three or four that stand out.

In my upright INFJ *Happy Head* image, I like the phrases 'work with integrity', 'motivate others', 'seek meaning', 'compassion', and 'encourage harmony'. These words capture what a good day would mean to me. On working days when I can use aspects of my *Happy Head*, I will be delighted with my work.

In my upside-down INFJ *Stress Head* image, I like the phrases 'negativity from others', 'ideas met with criticism', and 'not being appreciated for making a difference'. These phrases describe the terrible days I have had in my working life. I try to avoid these types of situations now.

I continue to use MBTI in my coaching and capture clients' Personality Types, strengths, and *Happy Heads* in their coaching plans. It's one of the easiest ways to remind yourself what brings you joy and fulfilment.

Highlights

- Your personality is the way your consistently interact with the world.
- Myers-Briggs Type Indicator is a popular and well-regarded Personality Test
- It can tell you your strengths and weaknesses, plus what makes you happy and what makes you stressed.
- It is one of the easiest ways to discover what brings you joy and fulfilment.
- Managers can use it to work out when their team is at their happiest and best.

8

Find Your Zone of Genius

"Find a job you love, and you will never have to work a day in your life."

Mark Twain

Natalie had run through the rain to her car just in time to start our virtual coaching session. Her delay forced her to dial in on her mobile instead of logging in from home as planned.

I happily took the call while she remained parked. It took a few minutes for her to get settled. She apologised several times for being in her car, and I reassured her it was absolutely fine. I could see her, and the signal was strong.

Her company had put Natalie forward for coaching as part of a People Development Programme. They sold agricultural products. The goal was to allow Natalie to grow as an account manager. She had leadership potential.

Her parents had a sheep farm near Wrexham, North Wales, and she helped out after work. At times, she would go through the night to help with lambing. I was surprised that she was cheerful and sprightly during our sessions after such nights.

She was enthusiastic about the products she was selling. She knew first-hand how it helped farmers.

In past sessions, Natalie had entertained me with stories about cheerful Charlie and Kaleb, two characters she hung out with. I had seen those two on TV as part of a popular series called *Clarkson's Farm.*

I knew nothing about farming, but that programme opened my eyes. It's a brutal existence, with stupid long hours and you are in the hands of the weather gods. You are lucky to make a profit. I admired Natalie and her family for being in this industry. Today, there was a high energy around her.

"What have you been up to?" I asked.

"I have just had the most amazing afternoon. I'm on my way back from a client's farm. He struggled with his lambs, and our milk powder will really help him," Natalie beamed.

"How wonderful. Shame about the weather, though. You looked drenched."

"I know. It just started raining now. I got caught in the rain on the way back to the car. No matter," Natalie shrugged her shoulders.

"Okay. What's on the agenda for today?"

"I thought maybe we could talk about my current role. As you know, I'm not sure about it and want to explore options. I feel I'm over-thinking it a bit," Natalie responded.

"Good topic. I have an exercise to help you get clear about what option would suit you best. It's called *Zone of Genius*."

Note: You will find the exercise under **Resources,** at the end of the book.

"Sounds good."

"A coach called Gay Hendricks designed the *Zone of Genius* concept. In his book *The Big Leap*, Hendricks describes how, in life and at work, we move between four zones: Your *Zone of Incompetence,* your *Zone of Competence,* your *Zone of Excellence* and your *Zone of Genius.*

We are happiest when we spend more time on activities that we love and are uniquely good at. Ideally, we let go of those things we are not good at or are not enjoying."

I continued, "So, let's start with the your *Zone of Incompetence.* These are the things you do that pay that much attention to because they bore you and you are no good at this. For me, it's Pivot Tables. I always asked somebody to help me because I was no good at them."

"Ah, yes! For me, it's V-Lookups. I have always hated them," Natalie responded.

"In coaching, we always say focus on your strengths," I said, before adding, "If you can, delegate the rest. Next is your *Zone of Competence.* These are things you do well, but you are not the only one and you don't stand out. Also, you don't have that much interest in it."

Natalie thought and then said, "Writing technical articles. It's part of the job, but if someone else offers to write them, I'll be very glad."

"Okay," I said. "Let's move on to your *Zone of Excellence.* This is where it gets interesting. Gay Hendricks describes this as your *danger zone.* This is where you spend most of your time because you like it. Why do you think it's called the *danger zone*?"

"Because I won't delegate?"

"Exactly! It's your comfort zone. By constantly doing something you are good at you get stuck in a rut. You become *comfortably numb* and are not at your best. So, what's your *Zone of Excellence*?"

"Account management is where I spend most of my time. I think I'm good at it, but I don't enjoy it anymore," Natalie said.

"So, you are in your comfort zone?"

"I suppose so."

"Now, let's look at your *Zone of Genius*."

"Okay," Natalie said.

"You are at your best in your *Zone of Genius*. You are on a roll and doing something that feels naturally part of you. It doesn't feel like work and the day flies by. You are *in flow*, to use a coaching term. In this zone, you use skills honed over many years. It's unique to you. Nobody can touch you," I explained.

Natalie smiled. "I don't know… I'm not sure I'm a genius at anything."

"When are you *in flow*? When something comes so easily to you it doesn't feel like work?"

"I was today," said Natalie.

"What happened today?"

"I wasn't sitting in an office on a call. I was in front of an actual farmer, telling him about our high-grade lamb's milk powder," Natalie explained. "I know how good the product is, I use it myself."

“How often do you talk to farmers face-to-face?”

“Rarely. The last time was at a Farmers’ Show. I loved that,” Natalie smiled.

“What happened at the show?”

“We got a stand, and I talked about how I use our products on my farm. It was a great day out, and good for sales, too.”

‘Would your company allow you to do more shows?” I asked.

“I don’t know. I’m sure they would. We could get a stand at the Wales Show for around £150, but I would have to come up with a strategy.”

“Great,” I responded. “What were you doing at the show that nobody else did?”

It went quiet for a bit. I didn’t say anything, and this allowed Natalie to reflect.

After a while, I added, “What makes your heart sing?”

Another pause followed, and I could see Natalie thinking.

“That’s it, my *Zone of Genius* is lamb’s milk powder! I want to be the face of it.”

Natalie beamed, and I could feel the emotion.

“I could even move on from account management and become the growth lead,” Natalie smiled.

It was a magical moment. It was almost like the car was a safe bubble for Natalie to speak her truth.

I have goosebumps as I write this. I was genuinely curious and cared deeply about Natalie.

That day, I was in my *Zone of Genius*, too.

Highlights

- When considering career options, go for what you're naturally good at and love to do.
- When the day flies by, and what you are doing doesn't feel like work, you are *in flow*.
- Focus on your strengths and delegate the rest.
- If you keep doing what you are excellent at, you are in danger of staying in your comfort zone.
- Instead, aim to do the work where you have a unique ability and your heart sings - your *Zone of Genius*.

9

Be Your Authentic Self

"Where attention goes, energy flows."

James Redfield

In life, you meet some people who you want to support, unconditionally, because you are inspired by their cause. For me, Sharon, was one of those people. She was making her way in the world and was determined to succeed.

I first met Sharon at SoftwareOne. She came to London from our Singapore office and wanted to develop her IT consultancy skills. Because she was methodical, she soon gained a reputation for making complex topics easy to understand. She was a genius with data and our customers loved her.

What I liked about Sharon was that she was fearless. She was born in Ireland and, after obtaining commerce and law degrees, pursued opportunities abroad. It must have taken tremendous courage to leave Ireland and seek opportunities away from home.

It's in the blood of both the Irish and the Dutch to travel the world. I moved to the UK in my early twenties and leaving behind family and friends was one of the hardest things I have ever done. Without knowing all the circumstances, I admired Sharon.

She was ambitious and wanted more than the company could give, so she ended up seeking opportunities elsewhere. We lost contact for a few years until she reached out and asked me to coach her. I felt delighted. I had recently become redundant and started my coaching practice.

It turned out that Sharon had also started her own business, an SAP Consultancy, and was looking to grow it.

For those of you who are not familiar with SAP, it is a software solution. Large corporates use it to run their back-office systems. Finance, HR, Supply Chain and Sales Departments use it. The product runs report on budgets, payroll, inventory, customer relationships, sales performance and more.

Maintaining SAP products after installation is very time-consuming and costly. Frequent updates and changes in SAP technologies can make it difficult for IT managers to keep up. The licencing model and billing structure are very complex. There is often a shortage of skilled SAP professionals, making it a perfect niche for IT consultants. In short; The world of SAP is a minefield.

Sharon had carved herself a career in helping people through this. She had spent years learning about the technology and how to optimise both the contract and costs of running such a beast.

Sharon was very clear about who she was and where she was going. She wanted to use the coaching to create a business that represented what she stood for. This was about creating a legacy.

Sharon wanted to create a business that was aligned with her principles and grow it by inviting team members to join her. They'd benefit from her knowledge and approach. She was passing on wisdom to the next generation.

Our first conversation was a wonderful catch up. I heard about what Sharon had been up to and what she was doing now. It soon turned to her business.

"Why do you want to start a business right now?" I asked.

"It's been a long-term aspiration, and the timing feels right. I can give it the full commitment and dedication it deserves."

"What type of business do you want it to be?" I asked.

"Our ethos is; 'We Create Happy SAP Customers'. The complexities involved with licencing can make it very hard for organisations to navigate. Our intention is to make the complex simple and provide real and lasting value to our customers."

"Sounds exciting!"

"I want to build a business where people do a good job, get paid well and maintain a work life balance. This is not about having a business where your colleagues are your family. This is a business that respects you have your own family."

"Interesting," I said.

"I want the people who work for me to feel valued; that their time with me was a good time," Sharon said. "And ... I want to support equity, regardless of background. Everyone deserves a seat at the table."

"You have a very clear picture," I commented. "What's the driver behind this?"

"I'm very passionate about what I do," Sharon responded with a smile. I nodded.

"I think we've come a long way in terms of gender equality, but there is still room for improvement. I think it's fair to say that it hasn't always come easily for women trying to prove their worth in a male dominated industry."

"I hear you," I said.

"The more women succeed in this space, the more we break down those legacy preconceptions and pave the way for generations of talented individuals."

"Wonderful. Ultimately, what would your legacy be?" I asked.

"I want to be remembered for being loyal, fun, hardworking, and generous," Sharon answered.

"Your authentic self," I smiled.

"Yes. Also, I want to build something that I can sell, so that I can support myself when I get older."

"Shall we start with what you already have and build on that?" I suggested.

"Sure."

We made a start on our plan by finding Sharon's strengths. By looking at her personality (ESTJ – Executive) we found creating order, reliability and dedication to be strong points.

"I think structure is really important," Sharon said. "It's not surprising that my business offers clarity of what could be a confusing topic. I create structure, and calm for my customers."

"What's another strength?" I asked.

"I would describe myself as loyal, patient and reliable. When I say I will do something, I keep my word. This shows up at work but also at home," Sharon explained. "I'd call myself dedicated. Some call it strong-willed. I defend my ideas and principles."

We both smiled.

As part of the personality work, we looked at what makes Sharon happy. Her *Happy Head* has these phrases that resonated: realistic, efficient, organised and pragmatic.

As the coaching sessions progressed, we explored Sharon's personal values and linked them to her business. Her three core values were challenge, generosity and honesty.

"I embrace challenges. Setting up my business has been a huge but enjoyable undertaking," Sharon told me. "It's less about success or failure, and much more about being brave enough to take the plunge."

"How does challenge show up in your business?" I asked.

'Well, SAP licencing can be a very challenging topic," Sharon smiled. "I educate my customers. I'm not afraid of the SAP complexity and respect it."

We spoke about generosity next. Sharon said, "I suppose having my business allows me to embrace this value. I enjoy being generous, especially towards my family and friends. It feels nice to help others. It makes me happy. In my business, I will always be generous with my advice and aim to over-deliver."

"What about honesty?" I asked.

"At home, I can be very direct," Sharon shared. "Sometime too much so. But at least people know where they stand. In my business, I will be honest with my clients. For example, I would say 'I won't take you on as a client, if I cannot help you'. I won't rip people off and I want repeat business. That's so important to me."

We agreed Sharon would refer to challenge, generosity, and honesty in her sales and marketing material.

When we looked at her *Zone of Genius*, Sharon's unique strengths were licence compliance and consultancy. She was excellent at creating watertight negotiation plans and was uniquely skilled in making the complex simple. She excelled at building rapport with customers, making it her mission to ensure no one ever felt foolish.

"There really is no such thing as a stupid question. My job is to demystify complex concepts and present them to my customers in an easily digestible way," Sharon told me.

We agreed she should keep the *Zone of Genius* activities and, where possible, outsource other activities, like appointment setting, blog writing, SEO, and posting on social media.

Next, we focussed on what was going to help Sharon with winning new customers and what was standing in her way.

We create a *Business Success Wheel* and listed eight activities. Sharon scored them on a scale of ten to assess their success. For example, 'Prospecting' was a four, 'Having a clear offer' was a five, and 'Marketing' was a five.

We repeated this exercise three months later and saw that all these activities had improved to a seven. Our attention to these areas produced tremendous progress. *Where attention goes, money flows* as they say.

Not surprisingly, Sharon's strengths and values could be her downfalls too. Her reliability and loyalty meant that often she worked far too hard. She would jump on deadlines created by others and forgot to set boundaries. There was little time left for business development. Coaching kept her focussed. She kept her eyes on the prize.

It was wonderful to see that at the end of our coaching journey, Sharon was embracing her fun side. She had done a cruise to St Lucia, British Colombia and the Dominican Republic. She also started networking with user groups and focussed on her *Business Success Wheel*. I know she will make her business a success.

Highlights

- Starting your own business allows you to create what you stand for and is a perfect opportunity to leave a legacy. It requires commitment and passion.
- Being aligned with your core values helps you to craft a compelling offer and create a supportive company culture.
- Your *Zone of Genius* will point to what activities to keep for yourself and what to outsource to others.
- Measure progress. Where attention goes, money flows.

10

Getting Unstuck by Letting Go

"In the process of letting go, you will lose many things from the past, but you will find yourself."

Deepak Chopra

I was on a call with Suki. She had a neat black bob and a soft smile. Her room had a minimalist white décor. Suki was born in the Far East, grew up in Central Europe and moved to the UK to work in marketing and communications before starting her own business.

She was well-travelled, with an inquisitive mind and gentle manners. She was a mum to two boys in their final years of junior school. Suki was ready for radical change in her business and wanted to explore options.

She was a coach, mentor and trainer. Her business was thriving, but she had fallen out of love with coaching. The trouble was, most of her income came from one big corporate client. If she stopped coaching, she would lose her biggest source of income. Suki felt stuck.

When people work with me to get unstuck, I don't ask what they want. The answer is too hard. We first talk about what they want to stop doing.

Letting go, gives people the headspace to explore options, with no pressure to figure out the next step. The way forward will present itself in good time.

I have created a model called Stop / Keep / Start / Be. It is based on the work of Phil Daniels, an American psychology professor. He suggested asking three questions when seeking feedback from others.

1. What should I *stop* doing?
2. What should I *keep* doing?
3. What should I *start* doing?

My Stop / Keep / Start / Be model is not for seeking feedback but for getting unstuck. It replaces the *should* with *could* and adds a fourth question:

1. What could I *stop* doing?
2. What could I *keep* doing?
3. What could I *start* doing?
4. Who do I need *to be* to embrace these points?

Suki attended several coaching sessions with me and did the Stop / Keep / Start / Be exercise. This is how the discussion went.

"How have you been since we last spoke?"

"I've been reflecting on the previous session, and I feel energised," Suki responded. Last time, I had many big question marks, but now I feel more positive and clearer in my head. This simple exercise helped me to decide what's important."

"Great. What were your responses to each section?" I asked.

Suki laughed. "It was very funny. I only have one thing in *Stop*. Emotionally, I would like to stop working with my biggest coaching client because it tires me. After many years of working together, they are not developing further. It's very tempting to say: Hey client, I'm firing you, but it's not that easy."

"You have a lot of energy when you talk about this and you sound very certain," I observed.

"Yes. It's a very good point, Wanda," Suki said with a smile. "In my mind, I practice it. I imagine myself and ask how it would feel if I told the client, 'I don't want to work with you anymore.'"

"You have a big smile on your face," I said.

"Yes, it makes me happy when I visualise it. I just need to find a way to make it happen."

"So there's only one thing you're looking to stop?"

"Yes, it's very surprising. I really thought hard, and I had a choice of many things that I could stop, but there was only this one big thing."

Suki continued, "The other thing that surprised me was the *Keep* list."

"What's on that list?"

Suki looked down at her notes and said, "There are three things, all very important to me. First, it's working with international clients. I'm so certain of this. Second, I want to keep learning and maybe work in education."

"Again, you sound so sure about this."

"Yes. I feel very certain about the international role and a little less certain about education. What I don't want to do is return to marketing, HR or sales."

"Good."

Suki continued, "I'm currently working independently, and I enjoy it, so will *Keep* it. I've been considering how it would feel to be employed."

"How would it feel?"

"I'm not sure I'll like it. It would definitely have to be part-time. I'm experimenting with this thought."

"Okay. So, that's still in consideration?"

"Correct. It is."

"It's interesting, isn't it?" I observed. "You have different energy levels with the different options you are considering."

"It's a very good point, Wanda. Yes, I didn't think about that, but it tells me that some things are more important than others in the list of things to keep."

I watched her and summarised, "I'm picking up on your certainty around dropping your biggest client and working with international people. More so than working in adult education and working independently."

"Yes. That's interesting. This is allowing me to have a plan I can build around."

"What's on the *Start* list?" I asked.

Ski laughed. "I enjoyed doing this because I thought, Oh, wow, there are so many things I can start. The first one is personal development. I'm unsure what subject, but I want to do this."

"What else is on your list?"

"Networking and being more visible. Earlier this year, I was homeschooling, and my attention was obviously elsewhere. Now that the boys are back at school, I have not gone out much yet. I feel I really want to be out there again," Suki said.

"What would that give you?" I asked with curiosity.

"Meeting people can give me new ideas about what I may want to do in the future. It will allow me to be open to something new."

"Perfect."

Suki continued, "The last thing on my list is teaching. I would love to teach. I've been doing coaching, mentoring and training during the last few years. I'm not sure about the coaching, but I love the training. Teaching is something I would really enjoy."

"That sounds like a great transition."

"Yes!" Suki smiled. "Whilst I'm speaking to you, I remember I have been invited to help at the boy's school, and I could use this as a trial phase to see what it feels like."

"Sounds ideal."

"Exactly!"

I did a quick recap. "So, personal development, networking and teaching are three things on your *Start* list and it sounds like you are enthusiastic about all three. You want to make these happen!"

"Yes. That's a good realisation," Suki said.

"Together with dropping your biggest client and working with international people, these are the items that you feel most certain about."

"I am."

"Finally, who do you need to *Be* if you are going to embrace these?" I asked.

Suki smiled and said, "I need to be more of myself. I am international, after all. If I could feel more comfortable with my international background and be willing to try out opportunities already offered to me, I would move forward."

She continued, "I have to visualise this. Actually, someone has just asked me to be on a Podcast. They said I could talk about anything I like. This may be an opportunity to try things out."

"What sort of things?"

Suki thought briefly and said, "I can test what it feels like to talk about my international background and what it feels like to be authentic. I have found some insecurity about this. About having the right to be here and belonging."

Suki looked away, took a moment to think and continued, "I could use the podcast to explore this: What is my story, regardless of how I look?"

It was a powerful shift in the conversation. I paused before asking, "How can you be more of yourself?"

Suki nodded and said, "By feeling comfortable with myself and not changing anything. I like that angle. It makes sense that I use the podcast to explore this further."

"Sounds amazing. What's your next step?"

Suki was energised and said, "I'm going to plan the podcast content. Thank you so much for creating this awareness."

"My pleasure."

I smiled as we ended our session. Suki is such a talented person with so many strings to her bow. Motherhood was moving to a stage where her boys didn't need her so much, and I couldn't wait to see what she would do next.

As I write this, Suki has moved back to Austria and now works as a university lecturer in international management and intercultural relations in both Austria and the Netherlands. What a powerhouse!

Highlights

- If you are stuck, you don't know what you want. You create space by thinking about want you could stop doing.
- You then progress by thinking about what you could keep doing and start doing.
- The key to unlocking yourself is to decide who you need to be, to embrace these points.
- The more energy you feel and certain you are about each of these points, the easier it is to move forward.
- By being more like yourself, the easier your choices become.

PART THREE
MINDSET COACHING

11

I Have a Mindset Blindspot

"When you unlock mindset, you unlock potential."

Dr Jodi O'Dell

I couldn't believe it. I'd been a coach for seven years and had never heard of *Voluntary Behaviour* and *Productivity Orientation.* I was listening to Dr Jodi O'Dell in her Mindset Coaching training, and I loved every aspect of the course.

Jodi taught us how to use her profiling tool. It measured fifteen aspects of mindset, and the report was extremely thorough. As coaches, we learned to interpret the report and provide feedback on the results.

The tool measured fifteen aspects of your mindset, assigning each scale a score between 1 and 10. A score of 1-4 means something is interfering with your performance. Jodi called this an *Inhibitor*. A score of 5-6 shows that you could be in your comfort zone and ready for *Growth,* whilst 7-10 means you have a strength, or *Accelerator.*

Jodi explained, "But here's the twist: a score of 9-10, turns your *Accelerator* into a blindspot, or *Derailment*. This is where a strength turns into a weakness. The strength catches you out. You are not always aware of it, but it might be how other people see us."

"What? This is such an eye-opener," I told Jodi.

"An example of derailment is when your high level of self-awareness turns you into an over-thinker. You've become too self-aware and self-critical and sometimes struggle to draw a line and move on," Jodi explained.

I can recognise the self-critical part, I thought to myself. I did not know it came from self-awareness.

"Another example is when people talk about having a lack of work-life balance, or feeling stressed and overwhelmed. I suggest you look at their level of *Emotional Commitment*. A score of 7 or 8 shows a strong sense of belonging, but if it goes into 9-10, it is likely that they have over-committed themselves and that is their blindspot."

I wish I had this tool when I was coaching Hayley. I wonder what her score would have been; I thought.

Jodi continued, "With *Voluntary Behaviour*, we are looking at your preparedness to do extra things or take on additional duties. A score of 7 or 8 might show that you are happy and fulfilled at work and willing to help out. A score of 9 or 10 strongly suggests people-pleasing behaviour. It's hard to say no, and you may not want to delegate. It's likely that you don't want to upset anyone and have difficulty setting boundaries for yourself."

Ouch, that hit a nerve. It was like I was looking in the mirror. I thought to myself; Have I had difficulties setting boundaries for myself? Jodi is probably right. I remember my manager, Caroline, telling me not to volunteer for everything.

My biggest light-bulb moment came when Jodi was talking about *Productivity Orientation*. "A score of 7 or 8 shows up as having a drive and wanting to improve things. You may enjoy stretching yourself and strive for excellence."

Yes, that's me, I thought.

"But of score of 9-10 means you are over-doing quantity over quality. You have become a perfectionist and possibly feel things are never good enough. You are a hard taskmaster on yourself and those around you. People may find you demanding because it's difficult for them to attain your standards."

"That's you, alright." I heard Doug in my ear. I became quiet.

I can't believe that I used to tell everybody that I was an extremely hard worker, a bit of a perfectionist, and always happy to help. With my new perspective, I realise that these are the key ingredients for being an over-worker and over-pleaser.

I created a cheat sheet to get my head around the topic. I still use this today.

Scale	Measures	Accelerator	Blindspot
Self-awareness	Awareness of own thoughts and attitudes, plus the impact we have on others.	Invest in self-reflection, learn from mistakes, and have good awareness of the impact we have on others.	**Over-thinking.** Very self-critical and sometimes struggles to draw a line and move on.

Emotional Commit-ment	The degree to which someone feels emo-tionally attached to their work.	Strong sense of belonging and loyalty. Happy and content at work. Feeling productive.	**Over-worked** Lack of balance. Over-com-mitted. Over-whelmed and stressed.
Voluntary Behaviour	Preparedness to do extra projects and take on addi-tional duties and responsi-bilities.	Happy, fulfilled, and willing to help out where needed.	**People-pleasing** Difficulty say-ing no. Lack of delegation.
Productivity Orientation	Your drive, and desire to strive for excellence, or stretch yourself.	Driven, wants to improve, and stretch yourself.	**Perfectionism** Type of over-thinking. Never good enough. Hard taskmaster. Demanding.

Looking back at the Myers-Briggs Type Indicator test, I now realise that certain personalities have a tendency to over-please, over-think, and over-work.

ENFJ's feel responsible for the success and well-being of their team. They thrive on making others happy and often put others' needs before their own. Butthey also have a tendency towards people-pleasing. They can struggle with saying *no* because they fear disappointing people or disrupting harmony.

ENTJ's take on large workloads and push themselves to the limit, believing that success comes from relentless effort. However, they also have a tendency to over-work.

ESTJ's are driven by efficiency and success, believing hard work is necessary for leadership and achievement. As a result, they also over-commit. Looking back at my discussions with Sharon, this was definitely part of the challenges of running your own business.

INFJ's (me) have a deep sense of purpose and a strong desire to help others. Often extend themselves to meet others' need while neglecting their own boundaries. They are deeply empathetic. My blindspot is people-pleasing and over-working.

INTJ's have high personal standards and a relentless drive to achieve their vision. With that comes a tendency to over-commit and over-work.

ISFJ's have a strong sense of duty and loyalty. They feel responsible for maintaining harmony and ensuring everything runs smoothly. People-pleasing and over-work is their blindspot.

The same applies to my *Core Values* exercise. With my newfound knowledge, around mindset blindspots, I could see how values like compassion, equality, fairness, harmony and responsibility could turn someone into an over-pleasing.

Fairness, impact, innovation, integrity, learning, and respects could easily be part of the thoughts of an over-thinker.

Accomplishment, advancement, commitment, competitiveness, courage are determination, are all pointers towards an over-worker.

I came out of my Mindset Coach training with Jodi a different person. I no longer took the strengths and core values of my clients at face value. I was now looking at where they're over-doing it.

I had moved on as a coach and I hope you will recognise yourself in the stories that are to follow. They will address the reasons we people-please, procrastinate, second-guess ourselves, over-think and over-work. The reason we do this is that we are over-doing our strengths and core values. We have a mindset blindspot.

Highlights and Mindset Blindspots Revealed

- A Mindset Blindspot happens when a strength turns into a weakness. The strength catches you out. You are not always aware of it, but it might be how other people see us.
- Too much self-awareness can turn us into over-thinkers.
- Too much emotional commitment to our jobs can lead to overwhelm and lack of work-life balance.
- Being too prepared to do extra projects or take on additional responsibilities, could be a sign that we have difficulty saying no and have people-pleasing tendencies.
- Our desire to strive for excellence, or stretch ourselves, could lead to perfectionism and the feeling that we, or others, are never good enough.

12

Stop Salami Slicing

"Never negotiate with yourself."

Alan McCarthy

My good friend, Ilana and I met at work. She ran the Western European Legal team, and I supported her in my role as Head of Commercial. I was also her internal coach. We had stayed in touch after my redundancy, and we loved each other's company.

Ilana had moved away from London and now lived in Barcelona with her family. She had just resigned. I treated myself to a trip to see her. It was early April. The Spanish sun wrapped itself around me like a warm blanket. I closed my eyes, raised my face towards the sky, and took a deep breath. How lucky am I.

We'd spent the morning at The Poble Espanyol, a tourist attraction up a mountain in the western district of the city. It was very relaxing to wander amongst the contemporary art galleries, craft shops, and replica regional houses.

Both of us were ready for a sit-down and a proper catch-up over lunch. The restaurant was perfectly situated in a quiet back street and the food was stunning. In front of us was a feast of slightly charred green padrón peppers, a plate of thick mozzarella layered with vibrant red tomatoes, and a large platter of patatas bravas. The red checkered placemats finished the look.

"You look happy. Being a lady of leisure suits you," I said.

"I am. It's so good to see you. I've missed you," Ilana smiled.

"I've missed you, too." I raised my glass. "Cheers!" I sipped the cold Cava.

"So, tell me, what's the one thing that made you resign?" I asked.

"There wasn't one thing, really." Ilana looked away and gathered her thoughts for a bit. "I was exhausted."

"You were brave."

"I don't feel it. After you and Andy left, the place wasn't the same," Ilana said softly. "Also, the business had changed, and it's much more challenging. It's all about making money now. I ended up working very long hours and jumping through hoops. It was very frustrating."

I saw the disappointment on Ilana's face.

"How did your team react?" I asked.

"People were so nice. I almost regretted handing in my notice. I'm going to miss them."

"Of course you are."

"You know, they were lovely, but they were also exhausting. I would spend hours making sure they were okay. I neglected my own work and had to spend my evenings catching up."

"No wonder you were exhausted."

"I'm not sure managing people is my thing. In my next job, I won't have a team. Less work, more pay. I'll enjoy that."

“Cheers to that!” I smiled, raising my glass. “You’re so good with people; don’t write leadership off just yet.”

“I won’t. But I’ve learnt my lesson,” Ilana replied. “I will have a work phone next time and will not be spending many hours ensuring people are alright.”

“What else will you change?” I asked with genuine curiosity.

“I won’t take on a team without a proper promotion,” she said without hesitation.

I nodded.

“Anything else?”

“I feel I should have left earlier, but I kept on going. I’m worried that others will be disappointed in me for not facing the challenge. I always want to prove myself. I’m always telling myself to deal with it.”

“I get it. You don’t want to run away from the problem. You want to face it.”

“That’s what I did,” Ilana said. “For too long, and it’s made me angry and unhappy.”

There was a theme here. Ilana was giving everything she’d got, but felt others ignored her. She’d given too much of herself, in terms of both time and money. She did it to support the team and the company, but the price she was paying was too high.

“Have you heard of the phrase *Salami Slicing*?”

“No,” Ilana giggled, “What makes you think of Salami? I thought you were vegetarian?”

"No, I don't want salami, but listening to you made me think of it. It's a competitive negotiation tactic. I learned this from a negotiation trainer called Alan McCarthy, and I've used it myself," I explained.

"Hmm.... I've never heard of it," Ilana said.

"Let's say, I'm doing a big contract negotiation and have a long list of contractual terms I want to improve. If I listed all my demands at the start, I would never get them. But if I asked bit by bit, I would have had more luck. The first concession I would ask for would be something small (a little slice of salami). Usually, I would receive it, just like that."

Ilana smiled. "Go on."

"A bit later, I would ask for something else (another salami slice). It's slightly bigger. I would add that it is a *reasonable* demand. Again, they would give it to me just like that." I smiled with satisfaction, thinking back to my past successes.

"Really...?" Ilana queried.

"Finally, just as the deal is about to be sealed, I would interject, 'Just one more thing' (remember Columbo?), and I'd ask for yet another concession (another slice). By then, the salesperson can smell their very large order and will give away one more concession to complete the deal. Anything for a simple life."

"I get it," Ilana nodded. "By giving away slice after slice, there is no sausage left."

"Recognise yourself?" I asked.

"Sure."

"If you give away time and effort, it costs you, and you could get yourself a poor deal. It leads to burnout and misery," I explained.

"I *know* I do it! I'm a giver! And it's exhausting!" Ilana said, looking at her empty glass. "But how do I stop it? I don't want this conversation to end. Shall we get another drink?"

"Absolutely," I smiled.

"People-pleasing is what I call a blindspot," I explained. "You may not see it, but by being overly empathetic, helpful and agreeable, you end up working harder than anyone else. You've probably learnt from a young age that helpfulness and not upsetting anyone is a good thing."

"Hmm." Ilana was staring at her empty glass. It had all gone, just like her energy had disappeared.

I continued, "But now that you are older, this is biting you in the bum. You're being taken advantage of and because, deep down, you want to be accepted, you work harder and harder. The way to get rid of this is to set boundaries."

"How?"

"Like you're already doing. By having two phones, you separate work from home. Also, look at what you can control. You are not responsible for the happiness of your team. As a leader, you are there to guide and empower them, that's all."

"I do feel responsible for the happiness of others," Ilana said. "I'm an empath."

"Maybe that's why you over-please and over-work," I added.

"So, I shouldn't care, is that the answer?"

"No, care by all means, but tone it down a bit. You are enough as you are, and don't need to salami slice to be liked or accepted."

Ilana nodded and raised her glass. "Thanks for reminding me."

"Cheers."

Highlights and Mindset Blindspots Revealed

- Salami slicing is a negotiation technique that uses a series of small concession requests to produce a much larger result than one large request could produce. By giving away slice after the slice, the seller can end up with a poor deal.
- By over-giving, or people-pleasing, you give away too much of yourself.
- People-pleasing stems from a desire to belong and be liked.
- As a people-pleaser, you may make the following mistakes:
  - Thinking that harder work increases your chances of control or acceptance.
  - Believing that how much you do for others determines your worth.
  - Feeling guilty when others are unhappy or disappointed when others ignore your advice.
- This leads to:
  - Feeling drained, both mentally and physically, with no energy left for your personal life.
  - Feeling that you're letting people down when you finally say *no*.
  - Feeling disconnected from your company and no longer inspired by your work.
- You can fix this by:
  - Setting clear personal and professional boundaries. Define what you will and won't tolerate.
  - Developing emotional resilience. Managing workplace stress and pressure without sacrificing well-being.
  - Surround yourself with supportive people.

13

Ditch People-Pleasing for Good

"Self-care is giving the world the best of you,
not the rest of you."

Katie Reed

Anna was beaming. "I was having lunch with a friend the other day and she said: You are a bit of a people-pleaser, aren't you? I then piped up, No I'm not. I've ditched that."

"Yes!" I smiled. "Well done, you."

"This stuff works!" Anna laughed.

"Of course it works!" I said whilst polishing my nails on my shirt. I was feeling so proud of myself. My *No Regrets Coaching (NRC) Group Coaching Programme* was coming to the end of its first cohort, and I had created something magical. I'd put a lot of effort into creating a supportive group for women. This moment was one of celebration. The women in the group had grown, but so had I.

I'd worked with Anna at SoftwareOne. She left soon after I joined, so I never coached her at work. When SoftwareOne made my role redundant, NRC was the first thing I started as part of WvG Coaching. I was longing for a community of inspirational women. Anna was one of the first NRC members.

When she joined, she had just landed a sales role at a software company after her previous employer made her redundant. We had this unpleasant experience in common. She didn't need to explain to me that being let go makes you feel rubbish. It steals your confidence and the entire experience is very stressful. You worry about lack of money, and what you could have done differently. Everyone says, 'It's not personal,' but oh boy, it feels personal.

"Can you remember why you joined the group?" I asked.

"Oh yes, I wanted to develop my confidence and make my mark at work. I'd just started at my new company. I felt very frustrated in the last place, but I don't think that will happen here. This very much feels like my happy place."

"What caused your frustrations at the previous place?"

"I felt unappreciated and taken for granted. I was emotionally exhausted. It clearly was just the wrong company, but I think it had also something to do with my level of confidence and being afraid to express my opinions. It led to a lot of resentment. I was unsure how to change the situation."

"Well, that's all in the past now," I said. "I'm so pleased you invested in yourself and look at where you are now."

"I know, I hardly recognise myself."

"I've really enjoyed hearing about your progress at work over the last few months. Have you noticed how your manager keeps putting you forward for new opportunities?"

"I have," Anna said. "I have listened carefully to the feedback from both my manager and my mentor and realise that hard work alone will not get me noticed. I've been working on doing more networking and speaking to senior leaders. I'm now co-chair of the Women in Leadership Group and that's really helped me."

"I have loved hearing about you speaking to senior female leaders. They are not as scary as you think."

"I used to be terrified to go to people with big titles, but the co-chair position gives me a genuine reason to contact them. Everybody has been very supportive."

"No longer being taken for granted, then?" I asked.

"This company has never done that. I feel more confident because I've let go of the need to be liked by everyone. There is a high level of respect for everyone and with initiatives like Women in Leadership, they are allowing us to spend time on personal growth and learning."

"That's wonderful," I said. "What have you learned from your mentor?"

"I used to go to him for everything. Again, now that I feel more confident, I go less to him for minor questions. Instead, we talk about future projects. He pushes me and sometimes believes more in me than I do myself. For example, when I do a sales pitch or a product demo, I used to always ask someone else to do my demos. Now I do them myself. I've had to learn how to do it, but it was worth the effort. I feel confident to handle anything now."

"You look like you are loving your work."

"I am, Anna said. "I've fallen on my feet with this company."

"One of my favourite sessions was when we did your *Zone of Genius* exercise. Can you remember it?"

"Yes, very well," Anna smiled. "I made notes, but I don't need to look back at them, because this session sticks in my mind. We talked about how I'm very good at gaining trust. I'm open and honest with my customers and meet them at their level. If a tough conversation needs to be had, we have it. I'm assertive without over-explaining choices. My main strength is being human, and I'm willing to be vulnerable."

"Wow. That's a very concise and effective summary." We both laughed.

"Talking about vulnerability. The other session that sticks in my mind is the one where we looked at your *Upper Limit Problem (ULP)*. This comes from the same book as the *Zone of Genius* and we talked about how we all have unconscious barriers that stop us from having it all. Common signs of your ULP are that you downplay your achievements and deep down, you feel you don't deserve your success. Do you remember?"

"I almost cried that day," Anna recalled. "It was a deep conversation, but definitely a turning point. I can't believe that feeling undeserving has been such a large part of my life. Right from being a little girl, I have felt broken and unlovable. I don't know if my complex family situation caused this feeling, but I often felt like an outsider. That I didn't belong."

"In what way was it a turning point?"

"For starters, my feelings had a name, and it was nice to know that I was not alone. You know, I grew up with what I might call *good girl* conditioning. You don't make a fuss, are always kind and you help others, even if it means self-sacrifice."

"Okay."

"I used to help my mum with her small money-making projects when I had no interest in them. I now realise that being a *good girl* has not done me any good. The fear of disappointing people has haunted me my whole life. It's rubbish."

"Kindness on overload."

"Exactly, the dark side," Anna smiled.

"What made you almost cry?"

"The realisation that this has been going on for so long. Nobody has ever told me I don't deserve what I've got, but I feel it. It's ridiculous. I have been walking around feeling I don't deserve the success that I've worked for, or the love that I've received. That I don't deserve to be here."

"You deserve all the good that is coming to you," I said in a soft voice.

"Anyway, after that session I was aware of my ULP and kept saying to myself 'No more ULP'. Moving jobs really helped. I really enjoy my work and I have settled in and get great feedback. The company feels like home and I feel I belong."

"No more ULP."

"Right," Anna smiled.

"What's been the biggest impact of NRC?" I asked.

"Definitely ditching the people-pleasing," Anna smiled. "I used to agree to things to avoid disappointing others. I used to think that I'd let people down, unless I gave them everything I'd got. Even to the point of breaking myself. I hated saying *no*."

"Both at work and at home?"

"Especially at home. I felt bad for putting myself first and let guilt dictate my decisions. All I've ever wanted is to be part of a happy family. By being so focused on pleasing others, I lost sight of what type of family I wanted for myself. That's all changed now, thank god. I no longer feel guilty about prioritising my own needs."

"I'm so proud of how you've created a life on your terms," I said.

"Thank you. I'm feeling genuinely happy and fulfilled."

Highlights and Mindset Blindspots Revealed

- People-pleasers are overly kind but because they don't advocate for themselves, end up standing in their own way of success – a blindspot.
- As a people-pleaser, you may make the following mistakes:
  - Avoiding advocating for yourself and hoping your hard work will get noticed without you needing to be visible or vocal.
  - Fearing confrontation and avoiding tough conversations.
  - Agreeing to things you don't want to do to avoid disappointing others.
- This leads to:
  - Being undervalued and overlooked, which leads to frustration and resentment.
  - Loss of confidence and emotional exhaustion.
  - Not knowing what you truly want. By being so focused on pleasing others, you lose sight of your own goals.
- The best way to tackle people-pleasing is to:
  - Communicate assertively. Express your needs and opinions without fear.
  - Break free from being the *good girl*. Unlearn social conditioning that rewards self-sacrifice.
  - Invest in personal development and learn how to no longer feel guilty about prioritising your own needs.

14

Just Do It and Stop Procrastinating

"He who thinks too long about every step will always stay on one leg."

Chinese proverb

It was a chilly afternoon in November, and Caroline and I met for our first coaching session over lunch in a tiny cafe in Ripley, Surrey. We didn't live far from each other, and the village was right in the middle in terms of travel. It was the perfect place to have a private conversation.

I chose a homemade vegetable soup with an enormous chunk of granary bread, and Caroline had a salad. The table was so small that I had to finish eating and put aside my coffee before getting out my notebook.

Caroline had been my line manager, until she moved to a global role within the company. I admired her and missed working with her. I have never met someone as hard-working as Caroline. She was pragmatic, calm and very knowledgeable about the operational side of the business. She never complained and gave her all in everything she did.

She dedicated her spare time and energy to ensuring the development and safety of others. She served as a child welfare officer at grassroots football clubs and volunteered as a Street Angel to protect vulnerable people during their night out in the town centre. She also loved gigs and festivals.

Today was rather special. She had pushed me for years to pursue my dream of becoming a coach. She supported me and was instrumental in my becoming an internal coach at SoftwareONE. Today was my opportunity to give back.

"Thomas is at university, and I'm slowly thinking about what I want to be doing in the future. I fell into IT, which has done me very well, but I have stayed in the sector because it allowed me to provide for the boy and myself," Caroline explained.

"I would like to use our coaching to explore options and figure out what I want to do for the rest of my career."

"Wonderful," I said. "Coaching is the perfect tool for figuring out where you are going. By spending time on learning about who you are, you can design your best way forward."

In the following sessions, we examined Caroline's personality, happy head, and core values. All of these would be the foundational building blocks on which to build the next step.

Caroline's Myers-Briggs Type Indicator personality test results came out as ISTP. The "I" pointed out that Caroline would reflect on things and felt comfortable working on her own. She preferred to know a few people well. We were fellow introverts in a sales organisation.

The "S" signified her preference for grasping information by examining specific details first rather than starting with the bigger picture. She solved problems by working through every step until she understood them. This explained why she excelled at the operational stuff.

The "T" showed that she enjoyed making decisions based on facts. She looked for logical explanations and could see inconsistencies in complex data sets. Again, no wonder she climbed the career ladder in the IT sector.

Finally, the "P" meant she had a spontaneous approach to life. She loved the social part of her role. Caroline was the opposite of me. If we had a party after work, I would have the train timetable on me, and I would leave early to make sure I caught the train before the last one of the day. Caroline ensured she had a wonderful time, and if she missed the last train, would take a taxi home.

"It is ringing true in so many areas," Caroline said when I explained the results.

The ISTP *Happy Head* had four phrases that appealed to Caroline. They were 'self-determined', 'analytical', 'independent' and 'thrive on variety'.

"So, whatever you choose to do in the future, make sure these aspects are part of your work. They are the things that make you happy," I explained.

"That makes so much sense," Caroline said with a smile. "It's great to know that the role I have right now fits this perfectly. It validates that I'm doing the right thing. It's just the sector that I may want to change. The IT sector has lost its appeal. It's still a man's world and I don't feel I'm thriving."

"Okay, let's look at what inspires you," I suggested. "I have this exercise called *Find Your Core Values* and it will help you work out what brings you a sense of purpose. I often use this exercise when people are looking for a new direction or meaning."

"That sounds great," Caroline responded.

We discovered that *loyalty, contribution, challenge, spontaneity*, and *resourcefulness* were Caroline's core values.

“Loyalty has always been there,” Caroline told me. “I have developed long-standing relationships, and others can rely on me. When I say I will do something, I will.”

“Tell me about what contribution means to you?”

“It means generosity and service,” Caroline said. “I want to make a difference. With my volunteering, I’m giving back. That is very important to me.” Caroline’s core value of contribution did not surprise me. Contribution is one of the six human needs, as explained by Tony Robbins, and we had this need in common.

“What about challenge?”

I enjoy learning new things and expanding my horizons. My transformation project for the UK stretched me and I enjoyed the challenge. Maybe that is why we are having this conversation now. My current global role isn’t challenging enough.”

“That’s interesting. How do you know that challenge is missing?”

“The whole idea of taking this global role was so that I could travel around the world and experience new cultures. With COVID, we could not travel and connecting over Teams is not as engaging. I’m training colleagues all around the world on how to use our new systems, but I’m not feeling like I’m growing as a person.”

“Let’s keep that in mind,” I added. “Whatever your next step is, let’s ensure it provides you with enough challenge to make you grow.”

“I agree,” Caroline nodded.

“What does spontaneity mean to you?”

“It means that I have the freedom to pick up different projects at work. I enjoy having my hands in various pieces of the business without being restricted to making changes." Caroline thought briefly and added, "Also, travel is a part of being spontaneous and, as we already talked about, I'm not doing much of that now."

"Finally, what comes up for you when you think about resourcefulness?"

"For me, that means that I get a sense of achievement by helping people. Even if I don't know all the answers, we move forward together and my team, internal stakeholders or customers get to their end game."

"To summarise what we have discovered, your personality is a good match for an operational role, and you are currently relatively happy. However, your latest role is not very challenging, and although it gives you the freedom to pick your projects, it lacks travel. You like making a difference, and outside of work, you do this by volunteering. Now that we have a clearer picture of who you are, let's explore options."

"Yes, please" Caroline smiled.

"I'm curious. Thomas isn't graduating for a couple of years, so why is this coming up now?" I asked.

"I'm mentally preparing myself, I suppose," Caroline smiled. "I like to think ahead and work out the details well in advance. As Thomas's need for my support lessens, I look forward to what's next for me. It cannot come quickly enough, and I feel mental preparation is part of the fun. Maybe I'm a bit on a control freak too," Caroline reflected.

"Okay, so let's have some fun. If anything was possible, what would you do?"

Caroline was quick to respond, "I would go travelling and volunteer somewhere in Africa. Maybe work with animals. Something totally different."

“Hold that thought,” I said. “It’s the unspoken dreams that give us a clue about our genuine desires. When it’s no longer about the money, we make different choices.”

“Ain’t that the truth,” Caroline responded.

Shortly after our conversation, SoftwareONE had a restructure which led to the closure of Caroline’s department, and her role was made redundant. This was an opportune moment to get out of the IT Sector and look for something new. But ... before she looked for another job, Caroline used her severance package to travel.

The first thing she did was to visit South Africa, where she volunteered for nine weeks to support a marine wildlife company. Then she travelled with friends to Tuscany, Singapore, and Australia, where she visited Sydney, the Whitsunday Islands, the Great Barrier Reef, and Cairns. That got the travel itch scratched.

When she returned, we continued our coaching.

“Have you had a think about what sectors you might want to work in?” I asked.

“Yes, it will be something like youth work, the sporting world, or an environmental charity. I have looked at vacancies, but I haven’t applied yet. I’m having too much fun catching up with friends and being a lady of leisure.”

“There is nothing wrong with that.”

“The thing is, I have worked all my life to climb the corporate ladder so I can provide for us, and that meant I put my own needs low on the priority list. Thomas is doing great at Uni, and I’m close to paying off my mortgage. Maybe I don’t need to work for a little while.”

"How does that make you feel?"

"Like I deserve this. It's liberating. I'm enjoying my newfound freedom. On the other hand, being off work is not all it's cracked up to be. Most of my friends work, so it's a bit boring, and I even though I'm doing voluntary work, I feel I can do more to contribute."

"Do you remember the *Find Your Core Values* exercise we did? You need contribution and challenge to thrive," I reminded Caroline.

"I know. I keep looking at vacancies and cannot make my mind up whether or not to apply. There is always something in the job description that puts me off. What if I start and I hate it? Also, every cover letter and customised CV takes ages. And then you don't hear back. It's a little soul destroying to look for jobs. If only I could find the motivation to fill in applications."

"Do you think you are over-preparing each application and maybe overthinking every vacancy?" I asked.

"Absolutely, I have too many options and I now feel I'm procrastinating. I'm very good at thinking things through, but maybe this strength is not helping much right now. My indecision is frustrating me a bit. Financially, I don't have a deadline. No deadline means no decision," Caroline smiled.

"What would help you make a decision?" I asked.

Caroline thought for a little while and then said, "It's always been my pet hate when people at work were indecisive and slow to act because they weren't sure about whether or not it was their job. I would always tell them *Just Do It*. Maybe it is time to listen to my own advice and *Just Do It*.

"That sounds like brilliant advice," I smiled. "How about I'll be your accountability partner and check in next week to ask how many applications you've made? You can be mine and can ask about my business development activities."

"That sounds like a great idea. Let's do that. I'll speak to you next week."

Highlights and Mindset Blindspots Revealed

- Mid-life gives us the option to make different choices and change careers.
- The career you fell into is not always what gives you purpose and meaning.
- When it's no longer about the money, we make different choices.
- When there are too many choices and no deadline, procrastination can kick in.
- Procrastination is a type of overthinking, and a mindset blindspot. It leads to:
    - Delayed decisions.
    - Little progress and feelings of frustration.
    - Career stagnation and limited opportunities for growth.
- The best way to tackle procrastination is to:
    - Use your strengths and core values to guide your decisions.
    - Set yourself a deadline and *Just Do It.*
    - Use an accountability partner to stay on track.

15

The Triple-Check Trap

*"If you change the way you look at things,
the things you look at change."*

Wayne Dyer

"Have you ever messed up so badly that you got a complaint from a customer?"

"Not really, now that I think about it, never!"

I was having a déjà vu moment. I have asked this question so many times and I always get the same answer. Paul was no exception.

I'd been Paul's coach for over a year. He was doing well as an IT Delivery Lead, and he wanted to sharpen his leadership skills. He knew his technical skills alone would not make him a successful leader.

"I'd love to stop second guessing myself," Paul said in one of our sessions.

"When do you do that?"

"You know, when I need to review a contract for a complex migration. I go through the document with a fine toothcomb and then start again, looking at it for the second time, or even the third time, to make sure I haven't missed anything."

"Okay."

"Maybe there is a bit of *Imposter Syndrome* going on here. The feeling that you've got to your position by chance. That you don't deserve to be there."

"Paul, you deserve everything you've got."

"Hmm .... I know I double or triple check documents when there's a tight deadline. The people-pleasing side of me wants to help. Migrations are hideously complicated. If I rush things, it could bite me in the bum."

"Yes, we have spoken about people-pleasing before," I said.

"My ability to push back is improving. I tell my guys: Hang on, you only sent me these four hours ago and now you're pressuris-ing me to get it done and out of the door. I'm still taking my time."

"Right."

"Sometimes, even when I have sent a contract to the customer, I go back to check if I've missed anything."

"Had you?" I asked.

Paul smiled. "It's crazy, right? I might find the odd small thing and I'm always frightened someone will say, 'You should have spotted that. Who's approved this, for Christ's sake?' The thought of it makes me uneasy."

"Okay, you triple check the documents and rarely spot any issues. What would happen if you did?"

"If something comes up with the customer, we discuss and resolve it," Paul smiled.

"Let's say I've got a magic wand, and I can make this triple checking habit go away. What would your world look like then?"

"I would have more *me* time to reflect or study. I would have more peace of mind, and more energy."

"Anything else?" I asked.

"It would help me with my career growth, and I could spend more time with my team."

"How can we get rid of this habit? That's the question, right?"

"Yes, it is," Paul said.

"Let's consider this today. The first step is to be aware of your behaviour and to what extend it helps or hinders you."

"Yes, indeed."

Please finish this sentence for me: *I'm triple checking and ...*"

Paul thought for a moment and then replied, "I'm triple checking, and I avoid mistakes that bite me in the bum."

"What else?"

"I'm triple checking, and I create high-quality proposals."

"What else?"

"I'm triple checking, and I help my team look good."

"Okay," I said. "I see your need for accuracy and helpfulness is shining through. But have you considered that maybe your triple checking habit is also working against you? How about we say: I'm triple checking … and I have never found a massive mistake?"

"That's true," Paul said.

"Can you come up with an example where the triple checking is not such a good idea? We call it a *reframe* in coaching. Like: I'm triple checking, and I have also lost my focus time today."

"Oh, I get it. I'm losing, not gaining. Like: I'm triple checking, and I'm also losing an opportunity to connect with my team," Paul beamed.

"Exactly. Let's add a few more."

"I'm triple checking, and I'm also making myself feel less confident."

"Nice. What else?"

"I'm triple checking, and I'm depleting my energy."

"Yes, that's an interesting one."

"I see what you mean by the *reframing*. I'd read about the concept before, but they didn't explain *how* to do it. You need to look at what you've got to lose. Instead of listing positive things, I need to consider what the consequences are."

"You've been thinking all this checking is a good thing," I suggested.

"Right, and the reframe gives me a bit of a wake-up call and points to the negative things."

"Exactly. The next time you are about to double, or triple check a document, consider if it's worth doing. It could be. Especially if it significantly improves the proposal. If it doesn't, drop it."

Paul smiled, "That's the key word - *significantly.* I like this *re-framing* approach. If I ask myself, 'How many times have I triple checked and found something? Never. That's significant. Triple checking is a trap."

I smiled.

"The *reframe* is one way of getting rid of this triple checking habit. The other way is to look at failure in a different light. Let's say you didn't check a document properly. What's the worst that can happen?" I asked.

"The worst that could happen is that we lose a bit of money. But a lot of the times it comes out in the wash. The project manager gets hold of it and says, 'Well, it's not very clear'. We then send improved wording in an email with no need to change the contact."

"And …?"

"You know, it's never been disastrous. I've got good people, and even if we make a mistake, we learn a lesson, so we don't repeat it."

"Do you see, when you look at it this way, you'll soon drop all the double and triple checking?"

"I can," Paul said.

"We have done a *reframe,* and we looked at failure in a different light. A third way to get rid of the triple checking habit is to look for someone that inspires you. Someone who already does what *you* want to do. Maybe a colleague. Do you know someone like that?" I asked.

"Katharine, who runs the Global Team. I don't think she's a double or triple checker. She's someone I look up to."

"Imagine adopting Katharine's approach. How would that make you feel?"

"That's a good idea," Paul beamed. "I would definitely feel more relaxed and more confident. I'll give it a go the next time I'm reviewing a document."

"So, here you have it. Three ways to address your mindset blindspot, which ultimately this is. You are over-doing your strength of being accurate and helpful, but you've lost your confidence and energy."

"It just shows how damaging something small like that can be. I like the *reframing* and then looking for inspirational role models best," Paul said. "I will use this from now on and will tell my team about it, too. I'll keep you updated on our progress."

"I'm eager to hear all about it next time," I said, ending the session.

Highlights and Mindset Blindspots Revealed

- Double or triple checking is a type of over-thinking, and therefore a Mindset Blindspot.
- It stems from:
  - Fear of making a mistake or upsetting others.
  - Putting tasks and projects above *me* time.
  - Seeing the worst in every situation.
- This leads to:
  - Constant doubt which slows you down.
  - Over-preparing, which depletes your energy.
  - Questioning of your abilities, which erodes self-confidence.

- The best way to tackle second-guessing:
  - Reframe the behaviour.
  - See failure in a different light.
  - Model the behaviour of people that inspire you.

16

If Not Now, Then When

"Opportunities are like sunrises.
If you wait too long, you miss them."

William Arthur Ward

I was preparing for my first session with Adrian and read the company briefing. 'This programme is for the Top Performers in the company. It's a reward and an opportunity for further growth. Participants have a choice to opt in.'

My first reaction was, How wonderful! Companies often leave top performers alone, and it's great to see that coaching is being offered to support further growth. I'm looking forward to this.

Adrian was based near Amsterdam, and our sessions were online. I felt at ease as soon as he joined our first call. He was in his mid-forties, casually dressed, and worked from what looked like an attic room in his home.

The décor was light and airy. It reminded me of my mother's home. The walls, the staircase, the doors and the furniture were all white. This feels familiar, I thought.

Adrian told me he was married with three young boys. Earlier in the year, his brother had a stroke, and, in the last six weeks, a close friend had a heart attack triggered by diabetes. Both were in their forties and didn't see it coming. A bit like me, I thought.

The events shattered Adrian's world; they were his wake-up call. It had spurred him on to put family time and self-care at the top of his list. He was focusing on what made him happy and wanted to use his coaching to make sure he lived life to the full. I knew immediately I could help and was keen to hear more about his story.

"I play football with my boys four times a week and even trained as an official football coach. It's important that I do a good job. As a teenager, I competed in triathlons at national level and even in my thirties, I took part in Ironman races. I think I have always been driven." Adrian started telling me.

"I read you surpassed expectations in your performance review. Can you tell me about what you do?"

"I studied maths at university and my first job was in insurance. I joined my current company about eight years ago and I work as a software programmer. Our company provides financial software, and I would call myself an internal specialist."

"What do you like most about your work?" I asked.

"I get a buzz from helping people with complex questions. I can explain rules in a way others understand. I love brainstorming and am very visual. I enjoy handling a handful of large customers. My best days are when I can use my analytical skills and knowledge and make a positive impact."

"What is important to you, especially when you image the future?"

"My sons. I want them to grow up knowing I was always present. I had this when I was growing up, and I want my boys to have the same. My father worked for the government, which meant he started earlier and was home by four; just as I was getting home from school. I immensely appreciated that.

That's why I don't work on Fridays. That's the day I spend with my youngest son. We walk his brothers to school in the morning and spend the day doing puzzles or making things from clay."

"That's great," I said.

"When my youngest goes to school, I'll probably switch my working hours so I can be free on Wednesday afternoons. That's when all boys will be free. I want my sons, when they look back at their youth, to feel that I supported them in whatever they wanted to do."

"That's a very Dutch way of being," I smiled. "I'm aware of this trend of a four-day week for young fathers. It's called *Daddy Days*, isn't it?"

"*Daddy Days* isn't the term I would use. It's more for when your children are very young, and you get paternity leave. You get a four-day week temporarily and once your kids are older; you normally go back five days."

"I didn't realise," I said.

"Mine are between three and ten and it's a lifestyle choice. I permanently work a four-day week and want to maintain a balance between my work and my family. Luckily, my company allows this, and we can afford it."

"Thanks for explaining that. I can see your family is very important to you. What's important to you at work?"

"I have been thinking about this," Adrian responded. "I enjoy being a specialist, and it's important that complex questions get answered correctly. I also want to progress and that's important to me too."

"What made you think about this recently?"

"We have a reorganisation coming up. I'm wondering whether I'll have to choose between being a specialist or a manager. My team is only a few people now and I have no direct reports. I like it that way. Would I limit my progression if I stayed a specialist?"

Over the following months, Adrian and I pondered this question. Adrian was very knowledgeable about his specialist subject and enjoyed getting questions about it from colleagues. Tackling tough questions was his way of adding value. But can technical skills alone determine leadership success?

His personality test showed he was a quick thinker, excellent brainstormer, and charismatic. On the other hand, he could also be very argumentative and find it difficult to focus. Was he ready for a promotion?

Time management was a bit of a thing, too. Adrian told me, "I want to ensure each question receives a correct answer. It's important that no mistakes are made, as the consequences can be big. I overthink things and take a long time to compose my emails."

"We often link over-thinking to being very self-aware and concerned about how we affect others. It also stems from a tendency to avoid risks and being overly cautious. Overthinkers get stuck in analysis-paralysis and sometimes it shows up as not being able to move on from mistakes. They also say *yes* too often to avoid disappointing others. Do you recognise this?"

"Absolutely," Adrian replied. "I know my self-awareness is my pitfall. I'm more than capable of writing recommendations for the business, but because of the impact on our customers, I wonder whether maybe someone else needs to check it before it goes out. We have a tiny team and that could waste valuable time. I know that I over analyse situations like that and that slows me down."

"One way of tackling your over-thinking is to be curious about why you do it" I said. "What do you gain by having someone else check your work?" Adrian thought for a little while and replied, "I share the burden, I suppose, and we avoid mistakes. I'm more comfortable that way."

"Have you ever messed up?" I asked. "Not that I know of," Adrian beamed.

"Where else is over-thinking showing up for you?"

"I hate disappointing people and say *yes* far too often. My colleagues keep interrupting me with minor questions. Some days it's one after the other. I enjoy helping people. Often the thing I tell them allows them to get unstuck. That's a great feeling. But I'm busy and need to knuckle down, now and then, and I'm not finding that easy."

We talked about the pitfalls of saying *yes* all the time and the pressure Adrian felt to reply straight away. The lightbulb moment came when we looked at who inspired him and who could be a superb role model. Adrian felt his director was an excellent example.

"So, let's look at what he does and try to copy it," I suggested. "Well, for starters, he doesn't respond to my requests straight away, and that is fine," Adrian explained. "I can try to take longer to respond. By the time I do, maybe the problem has resolved itself." he added.

"Exactly, act like a director," I smiled.

A few weeks later, we met again. This time Adrian was working from the office, and he found a small meeting room for our call. Adrian looked down and shifted in his seat as if he had something difficult to say. "Can we change the topic for this session? Could we talk about what's happening today?" he asked.

“Of course. What’s up?”

“I need to decide today.”

“Decide what?”

“Whether I want a promotion to manager, with a small team. I can’t make my mind up.”

“How exciting. Congratulations. What’s getting in the way of your decision?”

“My friend.”

“What do you mean?” I asked with genuine curiosity.

“I work closely with a colleague, and I would call him a friend. If I take this role, it seems a bit like I’m choosing against him. It seems wrong. I don’t like it.”

There was a knock on the door and Adrian looked up. He had a slight air of panic around him. His head turned to me on his laptop screen and then again to the person at the door. I couldn’t see who it was. “I’ll be half an hour. I’ll come and see you then,” Adrian said with a nervous smile. The door closed.

“As you can see, I’m under some pressure.”

“Hmm. What do you need right now?” I asked.

“I could do with some good questions to guide me to make the right decisions.”

“Okay. How about we start with the friend? What would he want you to do?”

Adrian smiled. “He’d say, *Go for it*, but that doesn’t make it any easier.”

“Alright. Let’s look at this from another angle. This reorganisation. How often do these come along?” I asked.

“About every two years in my part of the business.”

“There are two questions that pop up for me,” I said. “First, we have spoken about not having any regrets in our previous sessions. It’s my go to checklist when I need to decide anything big. So, let’s see if this will help you. What decision feels more in line with living a life without regret?”

Adrian tilted his head backwards and looked up at the ceiling. It was as if he was accessing information and was checking in with himself. “I can still do this new role without giving up my Fridays, so I can keep my balance. I will still be able to work with my friend, but it will be less often. That’s okay. It’s a cool opportunity.”

He had a massive grin on his face. “I should go for it.”

“Let’s check in with the second question. If not now, then when?”

“That is such a good question,” Adrian responded in an uplifting voice. “I know these things don’t come along that often and, of course, I need to make the most of this opportunity. I had not thought of it that way until now.”

“Is this something you could use with your friend, too? I asked. “Maybe if you tell him about your decision-making process, he will fully understand?”

“I’m pretty sure he would be cool with it anyway, but yes, I could do that.”

We still had about ten minutes to go before the end of the session. I don't think Adrian would have changed his mind, but he was in danger of over-thinking things at this point. He needed to act and not procrastinate, so I said, "How about we finish our session a bit earlier and you talk to the person who knocked on the door and tell them your decision?"

"Would that be okay with you?" he asked.

"Of course! I think that is the best action you can take right now, and I'm looking forward to hearing about it the next time we speak. Go! Go now!" I urged him.

A few weeks later, I learned how Adrian had told the company that he was up for the new role. His management team was thrilled. His friend reacted equally supportive.

"What made the difference in our last session?" I asked.

"It was the question about 'If not now, then when?'. That made me realise I had to take the plunge. Thank you."

"No, thank you," I said with a massive smile on my face.

Highlights and Mindset Blindspots Revealed

- Your wake-up calls can come from nowhere.
- A four-day week does not stand in the way of getting a promotion.
- Over-thinking is a blindspot and causes you to second guess yourself. It prevents you from taking the bold steps needed to thrive.
- You can tackle a blindspot and change your mindset by doing the following:
  - be curious about why you do the things you do.
  - copy people who inspire you.

- The antidote to over-thinking is acting. The chances of taking action increase when you ask the following two questions:
  - What decision feels more in line with living a life without regret?
  - If not now, then when?

17

Every Perfectionist Needs a Best Friend

"Perfectionism doesn't make you feel perfect;
it makes you feel inadequate."

Maria Shriver

I love it when companies create Female Leadership initiatives. When I coach women on these types of programmes, my sessions often lead to deep conversations, and that makes my heart sing.

My sessions with Chantal were no exception. She had worked for her organisation, a global services company, for over twenty years and her current role of Client Services Manager saw her lead a team of fifteen direct reports. The company felt she was ready for her next career step. I was looking forward to hearing how Chantal felt about this.

An energetic mother to two teenagers. She was in her mid-forties and loved travelling the world, skiing, and going to the gym. The first thing I noticed was her large black glasses, just like Mel Robbins, and her welcoming smile. A modern bob highlighted her auburn hair, and her skin glowed. She oozed confidence and happiness.

We would soon find out that her confidence was only skin deep. You wouldn't have known. But.., I'm jumping ahead of myself.

Let me share Chantal's coaching journey and then you can see for yourself.

One of the first things we did was to look at Chantal's personality.

"You have come out as an ESFJ," I said. "That means others see you as outgoing and a people person and you prefer working in a group."

Chantal said, "That's true."

"The results show you are likely to focus on the details of a problem before looking at the bigger picture. When making big decisions, you prefer to decide with your heart and when we look at how you manage a team, you like having harmony and may be nervous when it's missing. Does that resonate?"

"Yes, it does."

"Finally, you are extremely skilled in planning. You plan everything in detail, and at work you rarely miss a deadline."

"That's spookily accurate," Chantal smiled.

"Now that we know your personality, we can discover your strengths," I explained.

I showed Chantal her test results and asked, "Out of the following statements, which two resonate the most? *Strong Practical Skills, Strong Sense of Duty, Very Loyal, Sensitive and Warm,* and *Good at Connecting with Others.*"

"Oh, I like most of them. That's hard. My top two choices would be a *Strong Sense of Duty* and *Good at Connecting with Others*. I think that's clear from my long years of service for the same company and I really enjoy working with my team."

When we looked at the Happy Head associated with the ESFJ personality, Chantal selected *Value Family, Down to Earth*, and *Harmonious*. These words described what made her the happiest.

"At work, having an amicable team makes it fun and I work hard to create an environment where we treat each other with respect," Chantal added.

We worked on developing Chantal's coaching and leadership skills. Her team was extremely busy and, at times, stretched. By becoming skilled in asking coaching questions, Chantal became more aware of where her team got stuck and what motivated them. Throughout these sessions, I felt we were getting closer, and I got a glimpse of a more vulnerable Chantal.

"I want to have a happy family, kids and team. It gives me energy. In contrast, the moment I see any of them struggle, I feel I step in too early and too often to help, and that drains me. I cannot bear it when there is an unpleasant atmosphere. I get far too involved in fixing things. It's exhausting," she told me.

"Which of your habits are sometimes more harmful than helpful to you?"

"I try my best to make sure everything is prepared and correct. I over-prepare for meetings and presentations, and spend excessive time improving emails, reports and slides. That can lead to doing long hours."

"Anything else?"

"I don't speak up much in meetings where there are more senior men in the room. I assume others are more capable than me, especially if they have a more senior job title than me. I have something going on with hierarchy, even after all these years in the company.

Also, I feel I should have it all together, so I overload my schedule with work, family and social obligations. I wish I could shut off my brain and feel less exhausted."

"I understand that this is exhausting. How would you like to feel more often?"

Chantal pondered for a bit and then said, "Energised. Empowered. Less stressed. In control of my workload, rather than feeling overwhelmed by it. Feeling proud of my achievements. Enjoying a sense of peace, knowing that I'm enough."

"The things you have listed often come up with perfectionism. Would you call yourself a perfectionist?"

Chantal laughed, "Oh yes, definitely. My perfectionism gets in the way all the time. If you can help me to get rid of that, I would be very interested."

"Let's work on that," I suggested.

A few weeks later, our opportunity presented itself. Chantal joined the session, and her energy was a little low. "I feel a little drained with work," she explained. "I've done this role for five years and I feel I'm standing still."

"Okay. Tell me more?"

"I've been thinking about moving to another team. I want to apply my skills and meet new people."

"How can you make this happen?" I asked.

"Actually, someone approached me for a new role in the company."

I was a little surprised by Chantal's answer. It sounded like a wonderful event, but she didn't look happy about it. "That sounds great. What happened?"

"The IT Director, who's known me for years, approached me about a leadership role in the Project Management Office. He needs someone with a fresh pair of eyes, and he thought I may be interested."

"Are you?" I asked.

"I don't know. I don't know whether I can do the job."

"The job of coming in with a fresh pair of eyes?" I asked, knowing very well that is not what she meant.

"When I started his job, I could look at it with a fresh perspective, and that helped me make significant improvements," Chantal explained.

"There you go. You've done it before. Can you do it again?"

Chantal smiled. "Of course I can, but that's not what I meant. What about all the project management stuff? That's all new."

"Don't you have a team of technical experts? What if they don't need you for that and instead are looking for a skilled leader and someone to improve the way the team works? Is that more likely?"

"Maybe."

"What else do you know about the role?"

"I believe it will be part of the Management Team, and I'm told that I can design the role for my needs."

"That sounds amazing. I'm not picking up much enthusiasm. What are your thoughts?"

“It’s not that I’m not enthusiastic. It’s just that I don’t know if I can do it,” Chantal said.

“Do you know anything else about how this request came about?”

“The Project Management Office team put my name forward. I know most of them and they asked for me.”

“There you go. Isn’t that proof that you don’t need to be a project management expert. They want you for your leadership skills,” I observed.

“I suppose I don’t like being judged.”

“Judged about what?”

“About my ability to understand everything about Project Management.”

“Didn’t we just conclude that’s not what they want you for?”

“I know. I just can’t shake of this feeling of self-doubt. I’m wondering whether I will be good enough.”

“Did you know there is a pattern of behaviour that perfectionists share? They have a tendency to be extremely hard on themselves. Far more than their manager, colleagues or friends. Over-thinking every decision exhausts them, and they’re frustrated with themselves for not being able to just relax. Is this what’s going on here?”

“Yes, you are right. I’m hard on myself. Far harder than I would be on my team members. I would never expect them to have to know everything on day one in a new job, but I expect it from myself. It’s mad. I would love to learn to trust myself in my decisions and let go of the fear of disappointing others.”

"Do you have examples where others have trusted you?"

"Yes. Plenty. My current manager is amazing. She's a powerful leader, and she has really empowered me since the day I joined her team. She ensured I received fair pay for my hours, and I'll never forget that. I'm not good at asking for things like an increase. She could see how hard I worked and didn't hesitate to organise a long overdue pay rise."

"What does this show you?"

"That others see more in me than I do myself?"

"What else?"

"That I should talk to myself as if I was a good friend or manager."

"What would your best friend tell you to do right now?"

"She would tell me to negotiate before saying yes to the current offer, and also to stop over-thinking things. Accept that perfection is impossible and unnecessary."

"Do you like that advice?"

"I love it, and this conversation has really helped. Thank you," Chantal said with a smile.

Highlights and Mindset Blindspots Revealed

- Perfectionism is a type of over-thinking, and therefore a mindset blindspot.
- As a perfectionist, you may make the following mistakes:
  - Expecting yourselves to know everything before taking action.

    - Assuming that others are more capable and confident than you are.
    - Over-preparing for meetings and presentation, wasting valuable time.

- This leads to:
    - Exhaustion from over-thinking every decision.
    - Missed opportunities because you wait to be ready.
    - Frustration at yourself for not being able to *just relax*.

- The best way to tackle perfectionism is to:
    - Learn to trust yourself by reminding yourself of how others have trusted you.
    - Treat yourself with self-care and compassion. Just like a good friend would treat you.
    - Accept that perfectionism is impossible and unnecessary.

18

High Emotional Commitment Leads to Over-work

"Regret 2: I wish I hadn't worked so hard."

Bronnie Ware

"I love my team, and I don't want to give them any more work, as it will stress them out," Sarah said.

"So, you would rather stress yourself out by taking on more?" I asked.

"I suppose so. Someone's got to do it."

I was coaching Sarah as part of a Women in Leadership Programme. She worked as a team lead at a global sportswear company and was in line for a promotion to manager.

She was in her late thirties, softly spoken, and friendly. Her family came from India, and she had lived all over the world before settling in The Netherlands.

That morning, she turned up to our session a bit frazzled.

"It's all happening," she told me. "I have two deadlines next week and I'm stressing out about it. I'm doing extra hours again and I'm not sleeping well."

"Can you tell me more?"

"I'm a team member down, and my manager is putting pressure on me. I'm dealing with very complex spreadsheets, and I'm finding errors, which means they need to be fixed before I can move forward. The system is slow because of the amount of data it is churning. I'm the last in the chain of people working on this data, and my manager expects me to fix it."

"What options do you have to tackle this issue?"

"I could go back to the team that made the mistake, and ask them to fix it, but I fear they will be slow, and we would miss the deadline. Or I could ask my team for help, but they already have too much work, and I don't want to seem incompetent. Or I could just get on with it and work extra, like I normally do," said Sarah.

"What makes you chose the option that creates work for you?"

"I know I will complete it to the standard my manager expects and can avoid any conflict, which you know is my go-to behaviour."

"Yes, I remember that," I smiled. "How do you think your manager sees you?"

"He's extremely demanding and I'm a safe pair of hands, I suppose. He can rely on me and knows things will get done."

"He's probably thinking you're killing it," I suggested.

"That's right," Sarah agreed.

"Do you think he knows that you're having trouble sleeping and are extremely stressed?"

"Probably not. I don't fancy telling him either, especially because we are talking about me getting promoted."

"If you could be totally honest with him, with no comeback, what would you tell him?" I asked.

"I would tell him the situation was a joke. We are not investing in analytical tools and are working in an old-fashioned way inside Excel spreadsheets."

"Go on…"

"I'm starting to feel that the price that I'm paying is too high. I'm frustrated that I'm the *go-to* person, but never the promoted one. I feel invisible despite working harder than anyone else."

"What you are describing is often associated with being over-committed. Do you feel that's the right description for what's going on here?"

"Yes, I'm over-committed, the company isn't."

"Being over-committed often stems from being too emotionally attached to your work. With your ESFJ personality, you are naturally very loyal and have a strong sense of duty. On a good day, you feel you belong, you love your team and you're happy at work. This is likely to happen 80% of the time."

"Okay," Sarah said.

"The problem occurs when that emotional attachment goes into overdrive, let's say 20% of the time, and you develop a blindspot. You cannot see it yourself, but your sense of attachment is out of balance. To protect your team, you end up taking on extra work, without pushing back, which causes stress and overwhelm," I explained.

"That's me," Sarah piped up. "It's probably fair to say, this happens over 20% of the time."

'On top of that, as we know, your ESFJ personality often makes you too self-less. To be seen as a team player, you go above and beyond and take on tasks outside of your role.

"Yes, that's true," Sarah said. "I fix problems, rather than have a conversation about it with those who were responsible."

"If you remember, when we did the *Core Values exercise,* you choose *Accomplishment, Determination, Loyalty* and *Recognition.* These are often associated with high performers, like you. It makes you an engaged and wonderful team member. The company is very lucky to have you."

"I hear a *but* coming," Sarah interjected.

"Exactly. But these values also drive overcommitment to your work. I you feel your achievements give you self-worth, you are likely to focus on productivity. Maybe you end up sacrificing exercise, sleep, or self-care because of workload. You could even feel guilty for taking time off, even when unwell."

"I recognise that," Sarah replied. "Only yesterday, I thought; Why am I doing this to myself? I'm exhausted. Why do I feel responsible for the company not investing in tools? It's just a job."

"Is it?" I asked.

"In reality, I will never look at my work as *just a job.* That's not how I tick. Everybody in my family is either a doctor or a lawyer, and here am I, feeling inferior being neither. I put myself under so much pressure to match my siblings. I over-deliver and over-prepare for everything, just to feel worthy."

"Okay, that's interesting," I said. "When you are not feeling worthy, what happens to you?"

Sarah thought for a little while, "I think I lose my confidence and start stressing out that I'm making mistakes or might get fired."

"Get fired?"

"Yes, you know, getting thrown out of the company."

"That's a bit extreme," I replied. "Okay, so we have established that you are working extremely hard, to protect your team, and keep up with your highly successful siblings. You stress about making mistakes and your confidence is sometimes low. How would you like to feel instead?" I asked.

"Less stressed. More chilled."

"Let's have a look at this. One way to change how you feel is to do what we call a *reframe* in coaching. In this case, we may want to look at how you feel about making a mistake. If you feel more relaxed about making mistakes, I predict you will feel less inclined to work all hours and therefore less stressed."

"Sounds good," Sarah replied.

"What do you think will happen when you make a mistake?"

"As I said, I will get thrown out. First out of the company and worse-case scenario, out of the country".

"Really?"

"Well, maybe we could survive on one salary if I lose my job. My husband has a good job, so we should be okay. I'd probably not get thrown out of the country. Sorry, I have a habit of catastrophising."

"I can see that," I smiled.

"You know, every time I drive my car in The Netherlands, I think I'm going to kill a cyclist." Sarah giggled.

"I get that. The cycle lanes are confusing. We were over a few months back and we accidentally stopped on a cycle path. We were lucky that a cyclist didn't crash into our car."

We both giggled.

"I don't think they would sack you after one mistake, so let's do a *reframe* on this. Let's view failure in a different way," I suggested.

"Okay."

"Let's assume, for a minute, that one of your team members came to you, and they'd made a mistake. How would you react?"

Sarah looked up, as if to recollect an event like this, and said "I would ask them what happened and help solve the problem. I would give her another chance to get it right."

"How many changes would you give her?"

"Quite a few. Three at least, and maybe more than that if I could see she really worked at it."

"Exactly," I said. "Can you see making a mistake leads to a discussion and a chance to correct it. You'd give her many chances before she's in trouble. You wouldn't sack the girl at the first opportunity."

"Yes, that's how I treat my team."

"How many chances do you give yourself?"

"One," Sarah smiled, picking up the difference between how she treated others versus how she treated herself.

"There you go," I said. "Do you think your manager would give your more than one chance?"

"Of course, especially when I remind him, we are a team member down. Oh, that's really helped me to be a bit more chilled. Thank you."

Highlights and Mindset Blindspots Revealed

- Being over-committed to your work is a blindspot – you cannot see you're doing it, but you take on extra work and it leads to feelings of stress and overwhelm.
- ESFJ personality types have over-commitment tendencies.
- Core Values like Accomplishment, Determination, Loyalty and Recognition all drive over-commitment.
- Over-committed people have the following incorrect beliefs:
  - Extreme loyalty leads to career success.
  - A team-player takes on tasks outside their remit.
  - Self-worth comes from productivity and work achievements.
- This leads to:
  - Chronic exhaustion from constantly overextending yourself.
  - Feeling invisible despite working harder than anyone else.
  - Guilt when you have to say "no", even when you desperately need to.

- The best way to tackle over-commitment is to:
    - Create boundaries around personal time, even if work demands it.
    - Clarify job roles and avoid taking on tasks outside your scope.
    - Reframe and view failure in a different light.

19

The Misguided Over-Achiever and Her Wheel of No Regrets

"When your heart speaks, take good notes."

Judith Campbell

'What's wrong with me?

"What do you mean?"

"You know, after working with me for five months, what do you see?"

"There is nothing wrong with you," I answered in a reassuring voice.

I was in an on-line coaching session with Drishti, a Finance Manager in a FTSE 500 company. She was highly intelligent and would describe herself as a high achiever, perfectionist and go-getter.

"You're redefining yourself. You're ditching self-criticism and perfectionism and have developed a knack for being more compassionate. That can be uncomfortable."

"I know, right? It's been hard the break the mould. I used to hold myself to high standards and dwell on flaws. I'm seeing a change in that and feel more relaxed."

"Wonderful. Do you remember our early sessions? I loved hearing your stories about living in different countries. I think your upbringing in India and your education in New York have shaped you to be who you are."

Drishti smiled. "I'm grateful for my experiences, but I know I have moved on. I want to be different from my parents. At the same time, I have a strong feeling of guilt. My parents want me to be close, but with me living in London and them in India, that will not happen soon."

Drishti was doing extremely well at work. Managers consistently commended her for both the quality of her work and her empathetic leadership. Her ability to build relationships was excellent, but after three years, boredom and a loss of motivation crept in. She was thinking about what to do next.

Rather than enjoying the successes at work, her drive and desire for excellence had got in the way of her happiness. She had taken her passion for high standards too far and it had turned into a harsh self-critic.

"My high standards made me feel like a failure and it makes me dissatisfied," Drishti explained.

"Well, perfectionism is a mindset blind spot. It gets in the way of your happiness," I explained.

"Too right."

"Constant overachieving isn't necessary. 80% is enough for a high achiever like you, as it equals 100% for others. By giving 80% to work, you could give more attention to hobbies and your relationship with your husband and your friends."

"I've never given 80% to anything," Drishti smiled.

"Try it," I suggested.

"I think a lot of my drive and perfectionism have come from my upbringing. My parents believed in giving me an excellent education, and encouraged me to learn as many skills as possible, so I would succeed in the corporate world."

"Okay."

"I started on this path and discovered that despite learning a manner of unique skills, I'm not climbing the ladder. I feel unsettled, and question the wisdom of my approach. I feel like the miss-guided over-achiever."

"How about we look at creating your own definition of success?" I suggested.

"Yes, please."

"You may have heard of the Wheel of Life exercise. You measure eight aspects of your life and give yourself a score between 1 and 10 for each aspect. If you score low, you're very unhappy; a high score shows you're thrilled with that life aspect."

"I've not done this before," Drishti responded.

"I have created my own version of the wheel and have called it the *Wheel of No Regrets.* It's based on the top five regrets of the dying. They are: I wish I'd the courage to live a life true to myself, I wish I hadn't worked so hard, I wish I'd had the courage to express my feelings, I wish I had stayed in touch with my friends, and I wish I had let myself be happier."

"Wow, that's some list," Drishti pondered.

"It is. My wheel has eight measures of success based on living free of regret. It focuses on living a life aligned to your values, with strong relationships, and making the most of every opportunity."

"Sounds great," Drishti smiled.

You can find my *Wheel of No Regrets* in the **Resources** section at the back of this book. How would you score yourself?
The wheel measures the following aspects:

1. *True Self*
   In everything that I do, I feel I can be myself. I do not feel any pressure to behave in a way that others or society demand of me and feel I can speak openly.

2. *Work-Life Balance*
   I don't prioritise work over loved ones. I have plenty of time for rest and hobbies. My work gives me joy and does not feel stressful.

3. *Express Feelings*
   I communicate my feelings to those that matter to me most. I can articulate my worth and communicate with empathy and kindness.

4. *Family and Friends*
   I nurture and keep strong relationships with my loved ones. I make time to stay in touch with friends and have good working relationships.

5. *Self-Care*
   I let myself to be happy. I take care of my health and practice self-compassion. I practice forgiveness and do not hold on to guilt, resentment, or anger.

6. *Values*
   I know and live by my core values. They drive and inspire me to be the best version of myself. I'm clear about my values and have a strong sense of purpose.

7. *Strengths*
   I focus on building my strengths rather than addressing my weaknesses. I delegate or drop tasks that are not part of my strengths.

8. *Following My Dreams*
   I don't let fear or doubt hold me back from going after my goals. I have a plan and take steps to make my dreams a reality.

Drishti scored the highest on *Express Feelings*. "I'm careful with my words when speaking to people who are important to me. With my team at work, I plan my communications and feedback," Drishti told me.

Her lowest scores were for *Strengths, Self-Care* and *Following My Dreams*. "I'm so self-critical that I don't see my own strengths as something special," Drishti explained.

"Why do you say that?" I asked.

"I feel everybody has my strengths and I'm the only one with my weaknesses. I focus on wanting feedback on those. I have high standards for myself and others. I get frustrated with incompetence. I worry I might be a bit too demanding sometimes."

"Why do you think *Self-Care* and *Following My Dreams* have low scores?"

"My physical health is pretty good. My mental health is less so. I have a North Star in mind but haven't acted on it yet. Unfortunately, I tell myself off for not having started. Self-compassion and forgiveness aren't my strong suits. Guilt about not achieving my dreams is a massive thing." Drishti responded.

"Tell me about your North Star."

"Apart from getting a promotion at work, my big dream is to have a YouTube Channel. I would love to share all my cultural experiences and give tips on healthy food and the best places to visit and where to eat around the world. I picture myself on camera, addressing the world. It would be fun and educational."

"That's a wonderful idea. What is stopping you?"

"I think unconsciously my YouTube dream feels selfish. My parents had a dream for me, but their dream is not mine. I want to focus on my happiness and well-being over my work, but I don't want to let down my parents by pursuing my dreams."

"How do think your parent would react if you told them about your North Star?"

"I'm not sure. My parents raised me to believe that you shouldn't put yourself in front of others. It's like in the book *Leaders Eat Last*. I'm content to eat last, provided there is food left at the end. I know that not starting my YouTube channel is making me unhappy."

"How could you let yourself be happier?" I asked.

"You know, it really hit home when you told me about the top five regrets. It's about letting myself be happier. I know I'm free to choose a life I want and that there are different ways to what my upbringing taught me, but I cannot sell it to myself. "

"Why do you think that is?"

"I feel so guilty when I consider what would make me happy. I'm incredibly grateful for the many sacrifices my parents have made for me. Letting go of their approval feels like I'm grieving. I know I have all the freedom; I'm just not claiming it. Even my husband pushes me to go for anything I want. Seeing the world has given me confidence, yet I find it hard to be courageous and choose what I truly want."

"How can you make your dream a reality?"

"I should remind myself of the context and importance of this. After work, I could start planning my YouTube Channel and make a list of all the content I want to talk about in my videos," Drishti responded.

"Perfect. Now is your time," I said. "Release the guilt and make choices that bring you joy. Your parents created a wonderful start, and now it's your turn to create a life on your terms. The *Wheel of No Regrets* is shining a light on everything that will help you be happy. Measure it, focus on what you want to improve, and I'm convinced that you will make progress."

"Thank you, that really helps," Drishti smiled.

Highlights and Mindset Blindspots Revealed

- Perfectionism is a mindset blindspot. It stands in the way of your happiness.
- As a perfectionist, you may make the following mistakes:
    - Feeling you must prove yourself, even after years of success.
    - Always giving one hundred percent, when eighty percent will do.
    - Neglecting personal passions and hobbies.

- This leads to:
  - Constant self-doubt, feeling like you're never good enough.
  - Guilt for not being able to "do it all" perfectly.
  - Feeling trapped in a cycle of always needing to do more.
- The best way to tackle perfectionism is to:
  - Let go of the fear of disappointing others.
  - Follow your North Star and embrace self-advocacy.
  - Use the *Wheel of No Regrets* to create a life on your terms

PART FOUR
RESOURCES

i

Find Your Core Values

Knowing your core values helps you to understand what drives you and what inspires you.

Don't think too much when selecting the core values. What comes to your mind first will be the clearest sign of your values.

Ask yourself:
What describes me best?
What did I learn from my parents?
What was I like at school?
How would my best friend describe me?

Please choose ten words that best describe who you are and that motivate you to be the best version of yourself. You already live by these principles. This is not about who you want to be in the future. If there are words missing, please add them.

Accomplishment	Advancement	Adventure	Commitment	Compassion
Competitiveness	Courage	Determination	Equality	Fairness
Family	Freedom	Fun	Harmony	Health
Humour	Impact	Innovation	Integrity	Joy
Learning	Loyalty	Order	Passion	Power
Recognition	Relationships	Respect	Responsibility	

Now cross out four and reduce the list down to six. Remove words that are similar or less important to you. Keep the six words that motivate you to be the best version of yourself.

Ask yourself:
Does this value boost my self-esteem?
Am I proud of it?
Would it feel okay to share this with others?
Does it represent things I would support, even if my choice isn't popular or would put me in the minority?

The next step of the exercise is to reduce the list of six down to your final three.

These are what I call your *Top Core Values*.

Note them here:

1.
2.
3.

These are the things you stand for, the things you would fight for, and the things that would upset you if they were missing in your life.

ii

The Eisenhower Matrix and Magic Quadrant

This is a time management tool designed by Dwight Eisenhower. He used it to help him prioritize and deal with the many high-stakes issues he faced as a US Army general, then as Supreme Allied Commander of NATO Forces, and eventually as President of the United States.

Quadrant 1: Top left. Important and Urgent. Do first.

Quadrant 2: Top right. Important and Not Urgent. Schedule.

Quadrant 3: Bottom left. Not Important and Urgent. Delegate.

Quadrant 4: Bottom right. Not Important and Not Urgent. Delete.

1. Important and Urgent.	**2.** Important and Not Urgent.
DO FIRST	SCHEDULE
Crises.	Proactive work.
Emergency meetings.	High impact goals.
Last-minute deadlines.	Creative thinking.
Pressing problems.	Planning and prevention.
Unforeseen events.	Learning and Personal Development.

3. Not Important and Urgent. DELEGATE	**4.** Not Important and Not Urgent. DELETE
Needless interruptions. Unnecessary reports. Irrelevant meetings. Other people's minor issues. Unimportant emails or status posts.	Trivial work. Avoidance activities. Excessive relaxation (TV, gaming, internet). Time wasters. Gossip.

When we spend a lot of time in one box, we will feel either stressed, calm and in control, frustrated or distracted.

We can shift our energy and productivity by moving from one box to the other. Ideally, you spend most of your time in the top right box (also known as the *Magic Quadrant*), as this is where extraordinary productivity occurs.

1. Important and Urgent. FEELING STRESSED	**2.** Important and Not Urgent. *aka The Magic Quadrant* FEELING CALM AND IN CONTROL
Burning out because you are running around, firefighting, all the time. This leads to mediocre performance. Some are *addicted* to urgency. Action: Move right. Start planning big goals.	These tasks move you towards your big goals, inside and outside of work. This is where balance and well-being are created. Block out time in advance for these activities. Action: Spend most of your time here.

3. Not Important and Urgent. FEELING FRUSTRATED Feeling that not much is being achieved, despite being busy. This could be caused by other people's requests or priorities that don't support your goals. Action: Say *no* more often and keep an interruptions log.	**4.** Not Important and Not Urgent. FEELING DISTRACTED These distractions lead you to being late or not finishing projects on time. They can leave you feeling tires, stressed and unable to be effective or motivated. Action: Consciously eliminate distractions.

iii

Choose Your Path by Journalling

Get yourself three soft-cover notebooks. Physical notebooks work much better than digital products. Treat yourself to pretty colours or patterns for the covers.

Give yourself time to write. Again, typing doesn't work so well. The movement of physical writing allows your energy to flow onto the paper.

Celebration Journal

Write down your small wins. These are all the positive things, successes, and celebrations, as they happen to you, no matter how small.

This could be 'I used my gym membership for the first time this month', or 'the family dinner was a great success, and I made my first homemade Yorkshire Pudding' or 'I got a pay rise'.

When you acknowledge and celebrate achievements, it significantly boosts your mood and overall happiness.

By writing them down as they happen, you will develop the skill of living in the moment. It shows you that you are capable. It inspires creative thinking and fresh approaches to challenges.

By recording how you overcame an obstacle, you will become better at finding solutions for future problems.

Read this journal on the days you don't feel it. This will keep you grounded and prepare you for when you must face challenges.

Evidence Journal

This journal allows you to reflect on what lessons you have learned and document evidence you are getting closer to your goals.

Write down the signs you got, what you saw, and how it made you feel.

A sign is anything that tells you that you are going in the right direction.

These could be 'I saw an advert for the company I fancy working for, and their offices are even more luxurious than I realised' or 'I saw a documentary that confirms that my next job role is in demand. I'm buzzing.'

If you cannot think of anything, these prompts may start you off.

- What achievement am I most proud of this week?
- What challenges did I face this week and how did I overcome them?
- Did I receive any feedback this week that made me learn about myself?
- What new skill did I learn this week and how did I apply it?

Write in the journal as soon as the 'evidence' happens and capture the feelings at that moment. Do not wait until long after, as the intensity of the feeling won't be there.

Read the evidence journal on the days that you are not at your best. The content will lift you.

BHAG Journal

The term *Big Hairy Audacious Goals* (or BHAG) comes from the book *Built to Last.*

BHAG projects create momentum, get people going and are stimulating, exciting, or adventurous.

Now, let's make YOU the project.

Write down what gets you going. These are the dreams you cannot calculate. The things that seem so far out there that you don't know how to make them come true.

What would you do if you knew you couldn't fail?

What is your bold vision?

If you have a goal, what would be your huge, daunting challenge? Like an enormous mountain to climb. Staying in your comfort zone does little to stimulate progress.

This is not about *things*. It is about *what makes you feel alive.* Things like meeting amazing people and having memorable experiences.

Writing in your BHAG Journal encourages you to flex your dream muscles. Most of us don't dream big enough.

iv

Discover Your Strengths and Happy Head

To Find Your Personality and Strengths:

Take your free 10-minute personality test here:

https://www.16personalities.com/free-personality-test

Go to your 16personalities results page and find your strengths in the left-hand tab, or type this into your browser: *16personalities INFJ strengths and weaknesses.* (Note: I'm an INFJ). Use your own 4 letters to find your strengths.

To Find Your Happy Head go to: *https://ap.themyersbriggs.com/type-heads* and download the Happy Head for your 4 letters.

The MBTI, designed by Katharine Cook Briggs and her daughter Isabel Briggs Myers, is based on Carl Jung's ideas.

I use this test in my coaching, and I have found it handy. I enjoy using MBTI because it is user-friendly and provides simple results. You don't need to be a psychologist or coach to interpret the test results.

Critics argue MBTI oversimplifies personality and places individuals into boxes that may not accurately reflect the complexity of human personality.

The word *type* in the Myers-Briggs Type Indicator is essential here. You have a preferred way of doing things (your type), but you can also behave in a non-typical way when needed.

V

Find Your Zone of Genius

Gay Hendricks, the author of *The Big Leap*, came up with the concept of *Zone of Genius.*

He found we operate in four zones:

1. Zone of Incompetence
2. Zone of Competence
3. Zone of Excellence
4. Zone of Genius

Let's discover your *Zone of Genius*, where you use your natural abilities to stand out from the crowd and you thrive in your work or business

What is Your Zone of Incompetence?	**What is Your Zone of Competence?**
What do you get negative feedback about at work? What do you do that just about everyone can do?	What do you do well, but so do many others, meaning your capabilities don't stand out?

What is Your Zone of Excellence?	**What is Your Zone of Genius?**
What are you tremendously skilled at? People cultivate this zone. It is practiced and established over time.	What do you love to do? What can you do for long periods without getting bored? In your work, what produces the highest ratio of satisfaction to time spent? What is your unique ability?

vi

Getting Unstuck with Stop / Keep / Start / Be

When you work with me to get unstuck, I don't ask what you want. The answer is too hard. We first talk about what you want to stop doing.

Letting go gives you the headspace to explore options without the need to figure out what the next step is. The way forward will present itself in good time.

I have created a model called Stop / Keep / Start / Be. It is based on the work of Phil Daniels, an American psychology professor. He suggested asking three questions when seeking feedback from others. What should I *stop* doing? What should I *keep* doing? and What should I *start* doing?

My model is not for seeking feedback but for getting unstuck. I replaced the word *should* with *could* and adds a fourth question:

1. What could I *stop* doing?
2. What could I *keep* doing?
3. What could I *start* doing?
4. Who do I need *to be* to embrace these points?

What could I STOP doing?	What could I KEEP doing?
What could I START doing?	Who do I need TO BE?

vii

Recognise Your Upper Limit Problem

In *The Big Leap*, Gay Hendricks explains why we sabotage our success: deep down, we don't feel we deserve to feel good all day, and we downplay our achievements. We have what he calls and *Upper Limit Problem*, or *ULP*.

Taking the leap means breaking the unconscious barriers that stop us from having it all.

These four feelings are unconscious barriers to success.

1. Feeling fundamentally flawed.
2. Feeling disloyal to family and friends.
3. Feeling you are a burden to others.
4. Feeling you must not outshine others.

Feeling fundamentally flawed

This happens when you believe that you are inherently broken or unlovable. Do you feel like you don't deserve the success or love you have?

- It's a myth! You deserve all the good that is coming to you.

Disloyalty

This happens when you fear that by succeeding, you are disloyal to family and friends. Are you worried about being disloyal to your roots and the people in your past?

- Your growth can inspire them! Celebrate your achievements and rise together.

Believing that you are a burden in the world

Some people feel that achieving more will add pressure and responsibility, and therefore a burden, to others. Do you feel a need to lower your success so that you won't be a burden?

- Shift your mindset! View success as a chance to create a positive impact, not a burden.

The crime of outshining

Some people have the false belief that we must dim our brilliance so that we won't outshine others. Are you hesitant to shine too brightly?

- Your light is needed! Shine at your brightest and inspire others to do the same.

viii

Wheel of No Regrets

One of my favourite books is *The Top Five Regrets of the Dying* by Bronnie Ware. She recalls the deep conversations she had with her palliative patients. Bronnie was excellent at listening, and this allowed her patients to be honest about their impending departure.

Bronnie's stories are both sad and funny and interlaced with her own struggles in life. The book shows how, when people have little to lose; they become free from societal pressures and empowered to speak their minds.

Bronnie found that our Top Five Regrets are:

- I wish I'd the courage to live a life true to myself, not the life others expected of me.
- I wish I hadn't worked so hard.
- I wish I'd had the courage to express my feelings.
- I wish I had stayed in touch with my friends.
- I wish I had let myself be happier.

I think Bronnie created a perfect foundation for what it means to have lived well. I took Bronnie's findings and started exploring what it meant to have no regrets. I built a *Wheel of No Regrets* Exercise as part of my coaching.

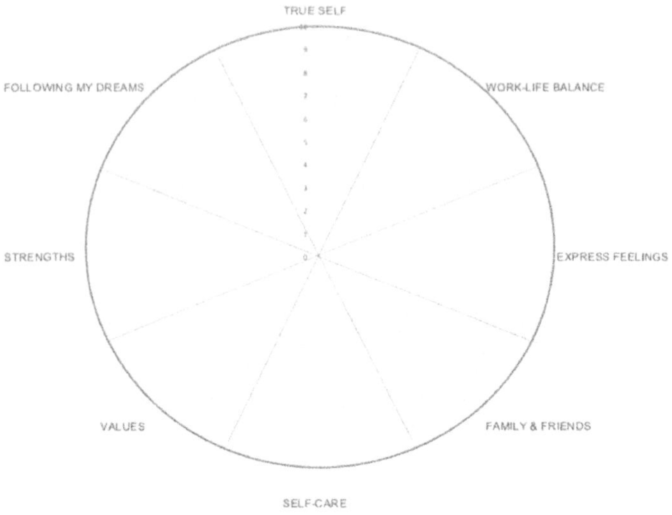

You measure eight aspects of your life and give yourself a score between 1 and 10 for each aspect.

0 = I'm extremely unhappy with this area of my life right now

10 = I'm extremely happy with this area of my life right now.

The wheel measures the following aspects:

True Self

In everything that I do, I feel I can be myself. I do not feel any pressure to behave in a way that others or society demand of me and feel I can speak openly.

Work-Life Balance

I don't prioritise work over loved ones. I have plenty of time for rest and hobbies. My work gives me joy and does not feel stressful.

Express Feelings

I communicate my feelings to those that matter to me most. I can articulate my worth and communicate with empathy and kindness.

Family and Friends

I nurture and keep strong relationships with my loved ones. I make time to stay in touch with friends and have good working relationships.

Self-Care

I let myself to be happy. I take care of my health and practice self-compassion. I practice forgiveness and do not hold on to guilt, resentment, or anger.

Values

I know and live by my core values. They drive and inspire me to be the best version of myself. I'm clear about my values and have a strong sense of purpose.

Strengths

I focus on building my strengths rather than addressing my weaknesses. I delegate or drop tasks that are not part of my strengths.

Following My Dreams

I don't let fear or doubt hold me back from going after my goals. I have a plan and take steps to make my dreams a reality.

How would you score?

Free Resources

I hope you have enjoyed reading the items in the resources section.

Please visit mindsetblindspot.com to get access to the extensive workbooks and other free resources.

Enjoy!

Download your Free Resources at **mindsetblindspot.com** or follow the QR Code

Acknowledgements

Writing my first book has been a two-year journey.

The first manuscript was a boring summary of my work as an executive coach. Then I met my publisher and editor, Paulin Prifti, and I joined his Publishing Mastery writers' group. Everything changed. I learned to tell stories and write more engagingly.

I want to thank my writer's group - Darren Mitchell, David Elston, David Harmony, Dorothy Dady, Francoise Falisse, Gillian Johnston, Jaques Smit, James Bateman, Jenny Adams, Kelli Binnings, Marco Puttolu, NicAnne Lamoureux, and Ouida Duncan, all skilfully led by Paulin. I can't wait to read your books.

Thank you, James Bateman, for being my proofreader. I've enjoyed seeing you develop into an amazing writer and cannot thank you enough for your input.

Then, of course, there are the heroes of the stories themselves: Adrian, Alison, Anna, Caroline, Chantal, Drishti, Grace, Ilana, Jack, Hayley, Natalie, Paul, Sarah, Sharon, Suki, and Zak. We may have changed some of your names; your stories are real. Without you, the book would have remained that boring first manuscript.

You opened up in my coaching sessions and showed your vulnerability. I'm extremely grateful that you have allowed me to share your deepest thoughts and self-development journeys.

Andrew Dunbar, Jodi O'Dell, and Melitta Campbell, thank you for the humbling praise. You've played an important part in my coaching and business journey. Your unwavering support has kept me going and I appreciate having you in my corner.

I've spent many an hour locked away in my study, and I couldn't have honed my craft without the support of my husband, Doug. We've missed out on time together and have skipped some of our lovely walks in the Surrey Hills. No more writing this summer, I promise.

References

Carnegie, D. (1981), *How to Win Friends and Influence People,* Simon & Schuster.

Collins, J. and Porras, J. (1998) *Built to Last*, Century Ltd, p. 91-114.

Covey, S. (2020), *The 7 Habits of Highly Effective People*, Simon & Schuster, p. 202-212.

DeLong, T. *Three Questions for Effective Feedback* dated 4th August 2011. https://hbr.org/2011/08/three-questions-for-effective-feedback.html

Happy Head: https://ap.themyersbriggs.com/type-heads

Hendricks, G. (2009), *The Big Leap: Conquer Your Hidden Fear and Take Life to the Next Level,* HarperCollins Publishers, p. 113-141

McCarthy, A. (2019), *Don't Lose it, An Ethical Guide to Resolving Everyday Conflict*, Frame

Personality Test: https://www.16personalities.com/free-personality-test

Robbins, A. (2001), *Awaken the Giant Within*, Simon & Schuster UK Ltd.

Slap, S. (2010), *Bury My Heart at Conference Room B, The Unbeatable Impact of Truly Committed Managers,* Penguin Books, p. 70-72.

Ware, B. (2012), *The Top Five Regrets of the Dying. A Life Transformed by the Dearly Departing,* Hay House.

About the Author

Wanda van Gelderen is an accredited mindset coach, who found her passion for helping high achievers to slow down and lead a life of no regrets.

Born in The Netherlands, she moved to the UK for her studies and remained after finding love. Wanda worked her way up the corporate ladder as an IT procurement leader in London's banking world. She negotiated massive deals with the likes of Microsoft, Oracle and IBM.

Then she had a heart attack, which forced her to take a step back. The hardest negotiation of her life had started. Her personal struggle to find a better solution became her inspiration to help others.

Wanda lives with her husband near Weybridge, Surrey.

You can find out more about Wanda and her coaching and training work at:

Website: https://wvgcoaching.com/

LinkedIn: linkedin.com/in/wandavangelderen

Instagram: a.coach.called.wanda

Printed in Great Britain
by Amazon

61929043R00102